# HUMAN CARGO

## POPULATION MOBILITY, MIGRANTS AND REFUGEES



RUTH NAUMANN

NELSON
A Cengage Company

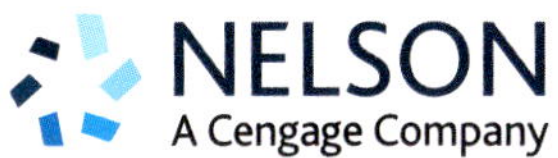

Australia • Brazil • Japan • Korea • Mexico • Singapore • Spain • United Kingdom • United States

**Human Cargo**
**1st Edition**
**Ruth Naumann**

Cover designer: Cheryl Smith, Macarn Design
Text designer: Cheryl Smith, Macarn Design
Production controller: Siew Han Ong

Any URLs contained in this publication were checked for currency during the production process. Note, however, that the publisher cannot vouch for the ongoing currency of URLs.

**Acknowledgements**
Image credits

Shutterstock: Images on pages 4, 5, 6, 7, 8, 9, 11, 12, 14, 15, 16, 17, 20, 23, 26, 27, 29, 30, 31, 34, 35, 37, 38, 39, 42, 43, 44, 50, 51, 52, 54, 55, 65, 66, 68, 69, 70, 77, 84, 90, 92, 93, 94, 96, 98, 100, 104, 105, 106, 110, 111, 112, 113, 114, 115, 116, 118, 119.

United Nations High Commissioner for Refugees: Images on pages 4, 10, 14, 18, 23, 26, 28, 31, 33, 36, 40, 91, 115, 117.

Alexander Turnbull Library: Images on page 72, Lloyd, Trevor, 1863-1937, Ref: C-109-003; page 73, New Zealand High Commission (Great Britain), Ref: Eph-A-IMMIGRATION-1912-cover; page 75, 04-07-1908, New Zealand Free Lance; page 75, Ref: 1/2-019148-F, Chinese gold miners with Reverend Alexander Don, outside a sod house at Tuapeka, Otago; page 77, Ref: DCDL-0009336, Malcolm Walker; page 78, Ref: DCDL-0030664, Martin Doyle; page 80, Ref: DCDL-0024526, Allan Hawkey; page 80, Ref: DCDL -0004953, Malcolm Walker; page 81, Ref: DCDL-0031165, Mark Winter; page 85, Ref: DCDL-0025623, Alan Hawkey; page 107, Ref: DX-002-134, Malcolm Evans; page 108, Ref: DX-025-118, Tom Scott; page 108, Ref: A-315-5-008, Malcolm Evans; page 111, Ref: DCDL-0009435, Malcolm Walker; page 120, Ref: DCDL-0006035, Chris Slane.

Other: page 34, US Navy (lower); page 45, Captain Croker, London, W. Hone, 1816; page 46, Don Quixote de la Mancha and Sancho Panza, 1863, by Gustave Doré; page 47, Newly arrived coolies in Trinidad, 1897; page 53, US Department of the Interior. National Park Service. Scotts Bluffs National Monument; page 54, 'Manifest Destiny', 1872, artist John Gast; page 56, Crossing the Mississippi on the Ice by C.C.A. Christensen, 1878; page 57, NOAA George E. Marsh Album, Historic C&GS Collection; page 57, family of five who are seven months from the drought area on US Highway 99. 'Broke, baby sick, and car trouble!', Dorothea Lange; page 59, US Dept of Agriculture; page 60, NASA (top), United States Coast Guard (bottom); page 63, NASA; page 71, Voyage au Pôle Sud et dans l'Océanie sur les corvettes L'Astrolabe et La Zélée, Jules Dumont d'Urville, Gide Paris, 1846; page 82, 'Landing of Convicts at Botany Bay' from Captain Watkin Tench's *A Narrative of the Expedition to Botany Bay.*
First published in 1789; page 83, Billy Blue, T.B. Best, 1834; page 87, US National Archives; page 89, US National Archives; page 96, US National Archives; page 117 (right), NOAA.

For product information and technology assistance,
in Australia call **1300 790 853**;
in New Zealand call **0800 449 725**

For permission to use material from this text or product, please email **aust.permissions@cengage.com**

**National Library of New Zealand Cataloguing-in-Publication Data**
A catalogue record for this book is available from the National Library of New Zealand.

978 0 17 038932 7

**Cengage Learning Australia**
Level 7, 80 Dorcas Street
South Melbourne, Victoria, Australia 3205

**Cengage Learning New Zealand**
Unit 4B Rosedale Office Park
331 Rosedale Road, Albany, North Shore 0632, NZ

For learning solutions, visit **cengage.co.nz**

Printed in China by China Translation & Printing Services.
4 5 6 7 8 21 20 19 18

# CONTENTS

# 1 What human migration is

Human migration is the movement of people from one place to another with the aim of living in the new place.

- Migration **to** New Zealand is when people from other countries come to settle in New Zealand.
- Migration **from** New Zealand is when people from New Zealand go to settle in other countries.

## Essential ideas to do with human migration

- Population is the grouping of people in places.
- The country into which the migrant enters is the receiving country or the country of destination.
- Since early times, people as individuals or family units or groups have willingly or unwillingly been legal or illegal human cargo as they migrate.
- Forced migration is when something such as war forces people to move.
- Movement from one country to another is international migration.
- Migration from one place to another in the same country is internal migration.
- The country from which the migrant leaves is the country of origin.
- Chain migration is a process of a small number leading the way to a new location and others from the same area following.
- Emigrants are people who migrate from a place and immigrants are people who migrate to a place.
- Migration has effects on people and places in both the country of origin and the country of destination.
- Voluntary migration is when people choose to migrate.
- Movement of people causes changes in population.
- Mobility is the ability of people to move from place to place.





ISBN: 9780170389327

# Randomly chosen news items about migration in one year

## 2016

An open letter to the British Prime Minister has been written by 145 celebrities and stars calling on him to allow migrant children stuck in a French migrant camp to enter Britain.

A man who was accepted into New Zealand from war-torn Syria says he wants to bring his three brothers and sister and their families into the place that feels like 'heaven on Earth'.

A Fijian in New Zealand, found guilty of immigration fraud, such as hiding his identity which included convictions for theft, has been sentenced to prison.

Pope Francis prayed at Mexico's northern border for the thousands of migrants who have died trying to reach the United States.

Sadiq Khan has become Mayor of London in control of a budget of $35.9 billion. He is the son of a bus driver and seamstress from Pakistan, migrants who came to London in search of a better life. Khan's new job makes him the most powerful Muslim in Europe.

Korean-born Lydia Ko, the New Zealand golfer who became the number one player in the world at the age of 17, has left to play in the Olympics in Brazil, saying she is proud to be a Kiwi and admitting that constant questioning of her loyalty to New Zealand has hurt. Ko became a Kiwi citizen at the age of 12. In 2012, *Time* magazine named her in its list of the 100 most influential people on the planet.

At least 22 Europe-bound migrants were found dead yesterday in an overloaded wooden boat off Libya. The Italian coastguard said at least 1800 migrants were rescued off the Libyan coast. More than 6000 migrants, mostly Africans in packed rubber dinghies, were rescued off Libya the previous day, while nine bodies were found.

Immigration New Zealand has sent its advice to Government on what New Zealand's refugee quota should be for the next three years.

ISBN: 9780170389327  

# SKILLS PRACTICE

1 **Being Curious** | Create at least five questions to do with human migration that you could find answers for to help you understand it better. Examples: From where did my ancestors migrate? How does migration affect me?

2 **Terms** | Give the terms for the following.

- **a** Movement of people from one place to another with the aim of settling.
- **b** Migration within the same country.
- **c** Migration from one country to another.
- **d** The country where the migrant came from.
- **e** The country where the migrant went to.
- **f** A person who migrates from a place.
- **g** A person who migrates to a place.
- **h** Migration because of a natural disaster.
- **i** Migration because of a desire to have an adventure.
- **j** Several groups from the same village migrating after each other to the same place.

3 **Decision-making** | Decide which one of the following posters you would use on a student notice-board to raise awareness about migrants. Give at least one reason for your choice.

4 **Assessing Current Knowledge** | Write a few sentences about how much you think you know about migration.

5 **Locating Examples** | Find and give examples of the following in the 2016 extracts.

- **a** Migrant wanting to set up chain migration.
- **b** Leader trying to help migrants.
- **c** Group asking Government to help migrant children.
- **d** Group of migrants whom New Zealand accepts under a quota system.
- **e** Types of boats on which migrants become human cargo.
- **f** African country from which migrant boats set off.
- **g** Kiwi sports star who was not born in New Zealand.
- **h** Immigration fraud.
- **i** Migrant's son becoming powerful.
- **j** War-torn country from which refugees escape.
- **k** Government organisation to do with immigration.



ISBN: 9780170389327

# 2 Push and pull factors

*Factor* = something that contributes to a result. *A factor in the movie's success was its teenage hero.*

*Push and pull factors* = a way of classifying reasons people have for migration.

## Push factors

= associated with the area of origin

= negative factors because they push people away.

- **Conflict** (e.g. fighting between Government troops and rebels)
- **Violence** (e.g. acts of terrorism)
- **Human rights violations** (e.g. not allowed freedom of speech)
- **High level of economic inequality** (e.g. wealthy minority, poor majority)
- **Persecution** (e.g. not allowed to practise religion)
- **Boredom** (e.g. looking for something new) 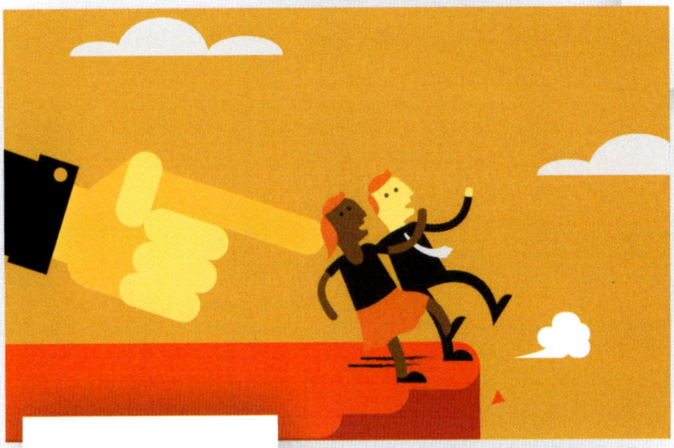
- **High crime rate** (e.g. organised gangs)
- **Poverty** (e.g. always worried about where next meal will come from)
- **Lack of economic opportunity** (e.g. no money to start business)
- **Natural disaster** (e.g. drought)
- **Overpopulation** (e.g. too many people for too few resources)
- **Few jobs** (e.g. no demand for particular qualification)
- **Bad government** (e.g. corrupt politicians)
- **Low wages** (e.g. depression in economy)
- **Lack of services** (e.g. little or no education)
- **Hopelessness** (e.g. feeling things will not get better)
- **Poor medical care** (e.g. no specialist care)
- **Desertification** (e.g. grazing land turning into desert)
- **Political fear** (e.g. opponents of Government imprisoned)
- **Poor chances of marrying** (e.g. more males than females in society)
- **Pollution** (e.g. lack of clean water)
- **Discrimination** (e.g. targeted because of religion)
- **Hunger** (e.g. famine)
- **War** (e.g. two countries fighting each other)
- **Environmental problems** (e.g. no official action to lower $CO_2$ emissions)
- **Slavery** (e.g. fear of being captured and enslaved)
- **Unwillingness to do military service** (e.g. compulsory at a certain age)
- **Lack of infrastructure** (e.g. no proper roads)

## Pull factors

= associated with the area of destination
= positive factors because they pull people in.

- Family members already there.
- Locals do not want to do low-paying jobs.
- Higher wages.
- Demand for labour to supply workforce.
- Able to earn money to send home.
- Good climate.
- Better chances of marrying.
- Government looks after environment.
- Better access to goods and services.
- Specialist jobs available.
- Lower risk from natural disasters.
- Political stability.
- More fertile land.
- Better housing.
- Religious freedom.
- New industries.
- Political freedom.
- Better education.
- Less violence generally.
- Advertising campaigns to attract migrants
- Less gang warfare.
- Better medical care.
- Better future for children.



 ISBN: 9780170389327

# SKILLS PRACTICE

1 **Creating Appropriate Symbols** | Create a symbol that could be used to illustrate the meaning of push factors for migration, and an image that could be used to illustrate the meaning of pull factors.

2 **Applying Terms** | Write a few sentences to go with each image to explain a likely push or pull factor.

3 **Sorting and Classifying** | Push and pull factors can be classified as economic (to do with money), social (to do with lifestyle and living in groups), political (to do with government), and environmental (to do with features such as air and water). Sort and classify all the push and the pull factors under those four headings.

4 **Analysing an Advertisement** | Examine the advertisement below and identify the following.

- **a** Date of publication.
- **b** Meaning of 'free passage'.
- **c** Reason for free passages.
- **d** Name of the company.
- **e** Receiving country.
- **f** Sending country.
- **g** People the advertisement wants to attract.
- **h** Two things the Directors will check up on for each applicant.
- **i** Location of Adelphi district.
- **j** Differences between it and a modern advertisement.
- **k** Time between advertisement and sailing.

5 **Photo Essay** | Create a photo essay — a series of photos, with or without text, that tells a story and is designed to create an emotional response from the viewer — of at least six photos about reasons people have for migrating.

**FREE PASSAGE**

**EMIGRATION TO NEW ZEALAND**

The Directors of the New Zealand Land Company hereby give notice that they are ready to receive applications for a Free Passage to their First and Principal Settlement, from Mechanics, Gardeners, and Agricultural Labourers, being married and not exceeding 30 years of age. Strict inquiry will be made as to qualifications and character. The Company's Emigrant Ships will sail from England early in September next.

Further particulars and printed forms of application may be obtained at the Company's offices.

By order of the Directors,
**John Ward, Secretary.**
No. 1 Adam Street, Adelphi (London)
June 15 1839

ISBN: 9780170389327  

# 3 Refugees

Imagine what it would be like to have no time to grab anything before you fled for your life because people were coming to kill you. Imagine what it would be like if you were being treated in hospital for wounds caused by bombs and had to pull tubes out of yourself to run away from more bombs. Imagine what it would be like to be so scared you had to get out of your own country. Being scared for your life is the reality for millions of people who become refugees.

## How the United Nations defines a refugee

'A person who is outside their country of citizenship because they have well-founded grounds for fear of persecution because of their race, religion, nationality, membership of a particular social group or political opinion, and is unable to obtain sanctuary from their home country or, owing to such fear, is unwilling to avail themselves of the protection of that country; or in the case of not having a nationality and being outside their country of former habitual residence as a result of such event, is unable or, owing to such fear, is unwilling to return to their country of former habitual residence.'

**The problem with terms**

The world uses the term 'refugee' in two different ways and this makes things confusing.

1. A general term for any person who flees because of fear for life. These people are also said to be displaced.
2. A specific term for a person given refugee status in the country to which the person fled and asked for refuge (asylum). The country or the international organisation in charge of refugees — the UNHCR (United Nations High Commissioner for Refugees) — has said yes, this person needs refuge and will be officially registered as a refugee and be able to get the rights given to refugees.

ISBN: 9780170389327

In 2006, there were 8.4 million UNHCR registered refugees worldwide.

By the end of 2015 there were 21.3 million registered refugees worldwide. Syrian refugees were the largest group. But if the general term of describing a person as a refugee was used, numbers would always be much higher.

Looking after refugees costs a lot of money. Towards the end of 2016 the EU (European Union — a group of countries located mainly in Europe, who work together as a political and economic unit) launched a programme to give out electronic cash grants to help refugees in Turkey, as part of a deal in which Turkey promised to cut down the number of people trying to enter Europe through Turkey's border. Refugees could use pre-paid cards to pay for food, education, housing and clothing and to withdraw cash from ATMs. Cards got topped up each month. Earlier, the EU set up a fund to help Turkey improve living conditions for about 3 million Syrian refugees in its territory.

## Taking in refugees

New Zealand has an annual quota of the number of refugees it will take each year. Up to 2016, its quota was 750. In September 2015 Government said it would take an extra 600 Syrians who had been living in Egypt, Jordan and Lebanon as registered refugees. In 2016 Government said it would increase its quota to 1000 each year. The annual costs to take on the additional refugees would rise by $25 million to $100 million per year.

**Registered refugees**
per thousand inhabitants in mid-2015 in countries chosen at random

| Country | Refugees | Country | Refugees |
|---|---|---|---|
| Argentina | 0.08 | Malta | 14.58 |
| Australia | 1.51 | New Zealand | 0.30 |
| Austria | 7.13 | Russia | 2.20 |
| Canada | 4.19 | Sweden | 14.66 |
| Chad | 30.97 | Turkey | 23.72 |
| Japan | 0.02 | UK | 1.82 |
| Jordan | 89.95 | USA | 0.84 |
| Lebanon | 208.91 | | |

Increasing numbers of refugees sparked off political cartoons and posters. Below are some examples of their clever messages.

*'You have to understand that people don't put their children in a boat unless the water is safer than the land.'*

*'How many people do you share a toilet with? In Zaatari Camp in Jordan there is only one toilet for every 50 Syrian refugees.'*

*'Treating refugees as the problem is the problem.'*

*'Shouldn't the existence of even one single refugee be a cause for alarm throughout the world?'*

*'A bundle of belongings isn't the only thing a refugee brings to a new country. Einstein was a refugee.'*

ISBN: 9780170389327

# SKILLS PRACTICE

1 **Personal Response** | Answer the following and give reasons for your answers. Should New Zealand be congratulated on its quota of refugees? Should it do more?

2 **Problems with Terms** |

Use the UN official definition to prepare an easier definition of a refugee. You could explain the difference between someone who is called a refugee in a general way and a registered refugee.

3 **Examining for meaning** | Study the graph and try to work out what it is about. Make some comments about it you can use in a discussion.

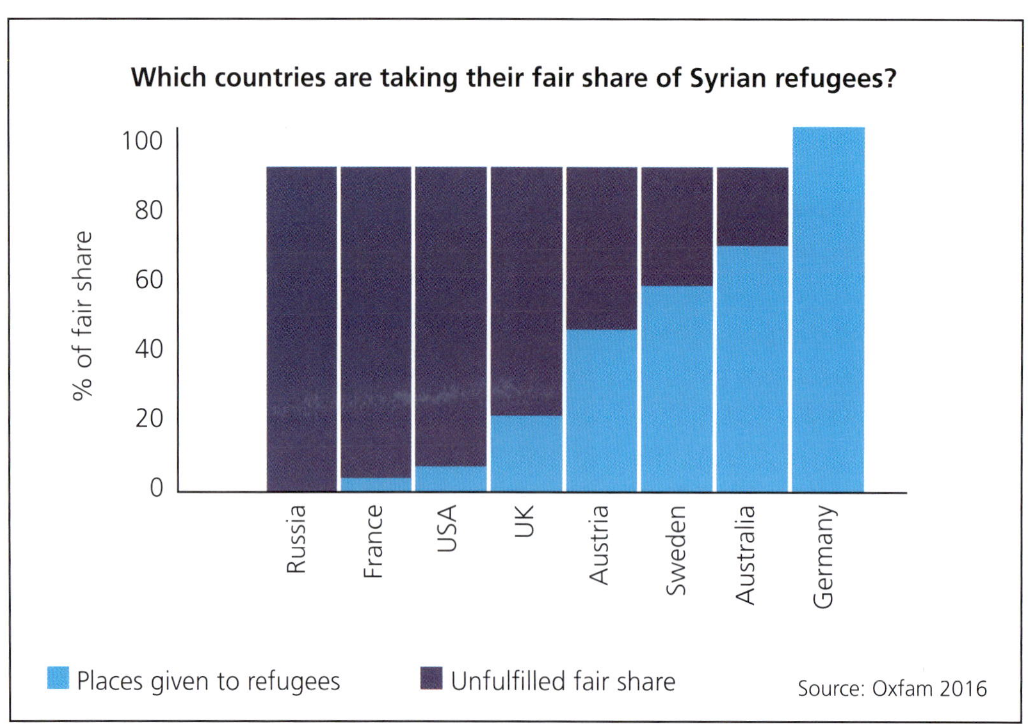


*At the same time as the United Nations met in 2016 to discuss what was going on in Syria to cause so many refugees, Oxfam (global charity helping the poor) published this graph. Oxfam worked out what funds each economically developed country should give to help Syrian refugees; the funds each country gave, relative to the size of the country's economy, was its fair share.*



 ISBN: 9780170389327

4 **Poster** | Either show a plan for a poster about refugees to raise awareness of the issue, or make the actual poster.

5 **PowerPoint Presentation** | These two graphics show aspects of a refugee crisis in Europe at the beginning of 2016. Choose data from them that you would use for one slide of a PowerPoint presentation.

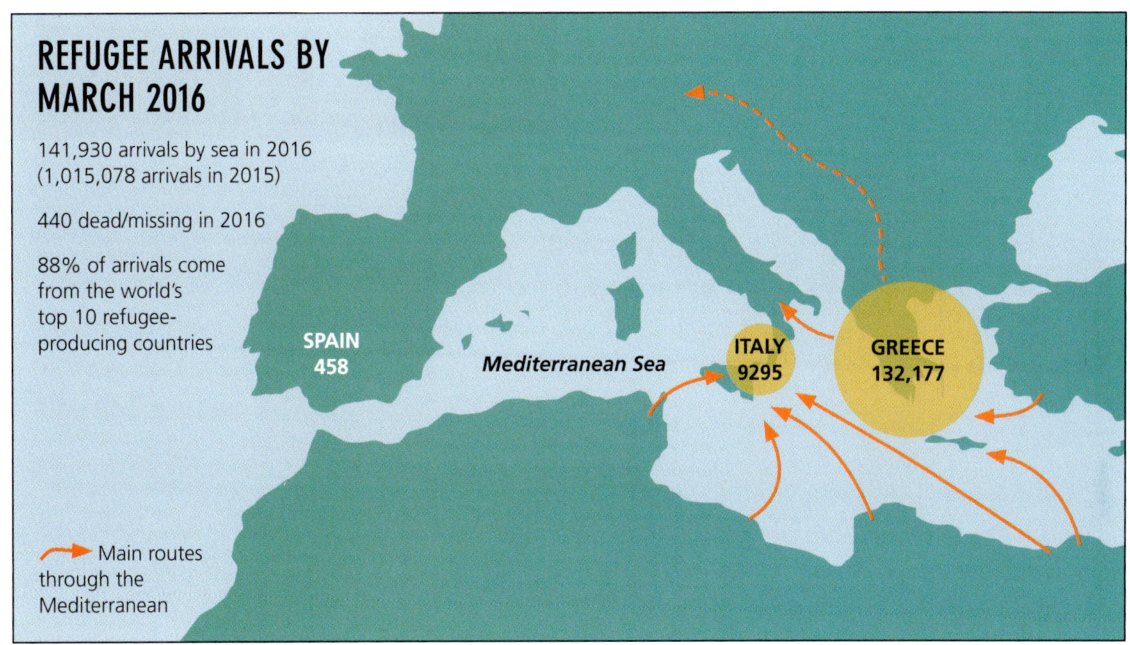


*More than a million refugees had entered the EU after crossing from Turkey to Greece by boat in 2015. Since Turkey agreed to stop people from setting sail from its shores, the numbers taking that route had fallen dramatically.*

## SYRIAN REFUGEE CRISIS FEBRUARY 2016

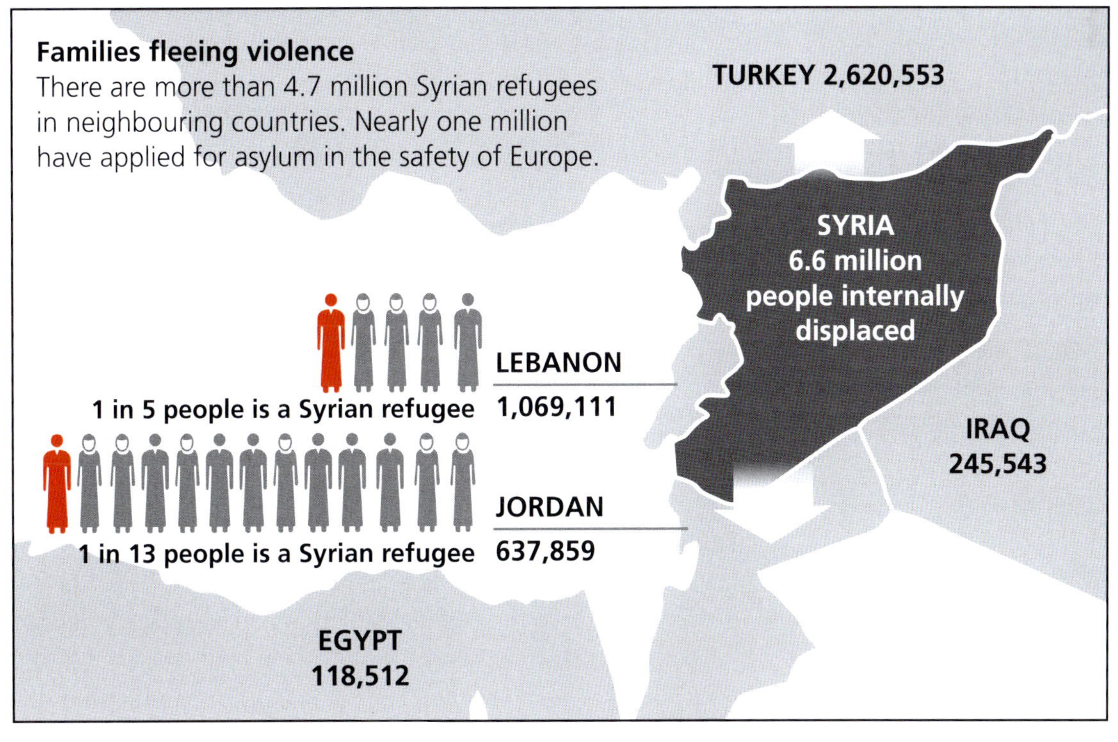


ISBN: 9780170389327 

# 4 Asylum seekers

*Asylum* = shelter and protection granted to somebody.

*Asylum seeker* = a person looking for shelter and protection.

**1** You flee your country because bombs destroy your house and kill your family.

**2** You need to find a safe zone, a place to shelter and protect you. You are an asylum seeker.

**3** You get to the border between your country and another country that does not have a war going on in it. It is closed with barbed wire and fences and soldiers are on the lookout. You manage to sneak across the border at night and find a camp of other migrants. You have asylum.

**4** The asylum is only temporary because you can't just creep in and expect to stay forever. You have to register yourself with authorities in this new country and apply to be allowed to stay there. Otherwise that country might deport you and send you back to where you came from.

Migrant Registration Centre

**5** You register yourself with the authorities and apply to be a permanent citizen.

**6** You go through a process and get given permission to stay. You are now called a refugee.

New Zealand is geographically isolated so it has never had a mass arrival of asylum seekers. But people who come to it and are too scared to return to their own country can ask for shelter and protection. They are asylum seekers.

A migrant can claim asylum when he or she arrives at an airport or a seaport in New Zealand by telling an immigration official or a police-person.

Officials process claims from asylum seekers and try to get them done within 140 days. New Zealand does not deport asylum seekers while their claims are being processed.

If the asylum seeker's claim is recognised, he or she can stay in New Zealand permanently. If not, the asylum seeker can reapply or must leave.



ISBN: 9780170389327

## The *Tampa* affair

In 2001, a Norwegian freighter called MV *Tampa* rescued 438 asylum seekers, mainly Afghanis, from a stranded Indonesian fishing boat in the Indian Ocean and decided to bring them to nearby Australia.

Australia asked the *Tampa* to return the asylum seekers to Indonesia. The captain refused and anchored the ship off the coast of Christmas Island, an Australian territory.

The Australian Government ordered special forces to board the ship.

Norway said Australia was not meeting its duty to distressed people on the sea. Australia said no asylum seekers were to enter Australia and introduced a system to take asylum seekers to a detention centre in the small Pacific nation of Nauru.

Australia loaded the *Tampa* migrants on to an Australian navy vessel and took them to Nauru. Australia later sent other asylum seekers there too.

New Zealand took about 150 of the asylum seekers. Australia received a lot of international criticism. Australian border control and national security became a hot issue for the Australian general election and the public re-elected the government.

## SKILLS PRACTICE

1 **Putting Yourself in Another's Shoes |** These shoes are on your feet. Describe how you feel.

2 **Process |** Outline a process that explains why the following statement is a fact.

*Every refugee has at some point been an asylum seeker.*

3 **Understanding Suggestion |** The questions about the graph ask you to 'read between the lines'.

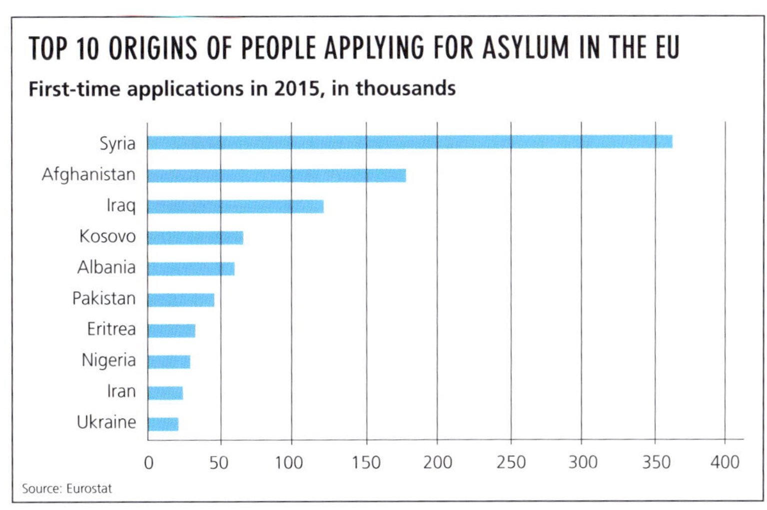

a What does 'first-time' suggest?
b What does 'Top' in the title suggest?
c What does 'EU' in the title suggest?
d What does the name of the source suggest?
e What does the presence of Ukraine in the list suggest?
f What does 'applications' suggest about the actual number of migrants in the EU?

4 **Structure of Data** | Explain how the following is structured. Think of format, use of symbols and text.

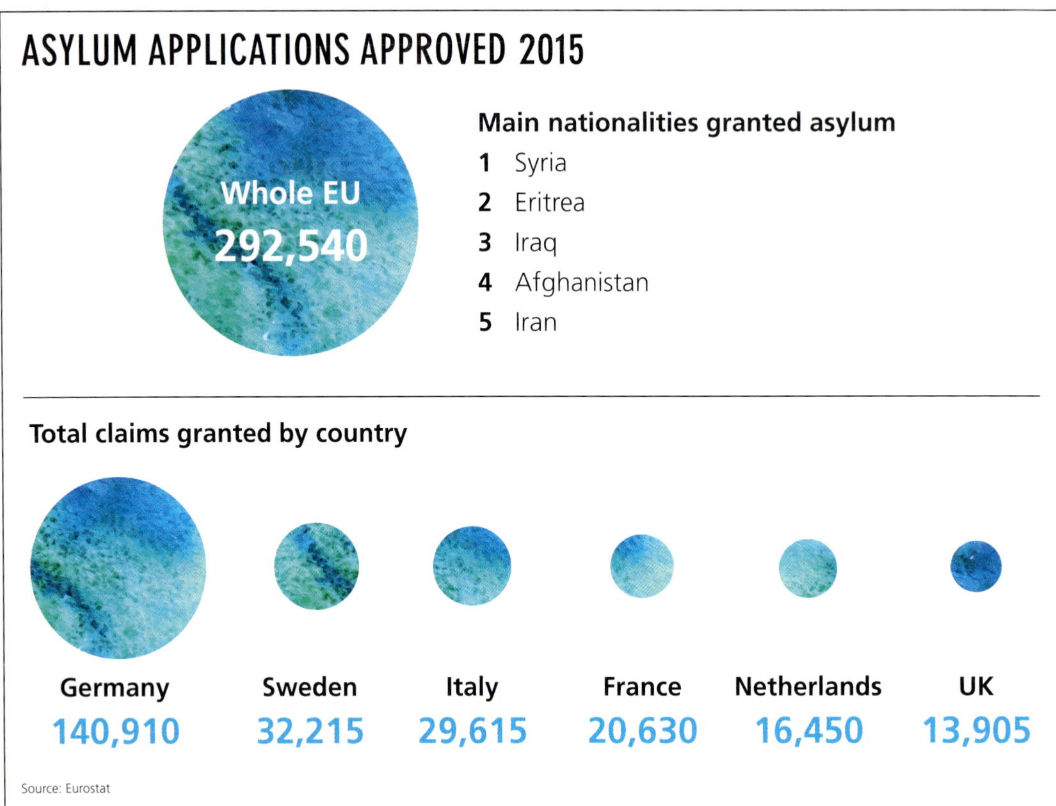


5 **Sorting Out Cause and Effect** | Make a graphic to show the causes and effects of the *Tampa* affair.

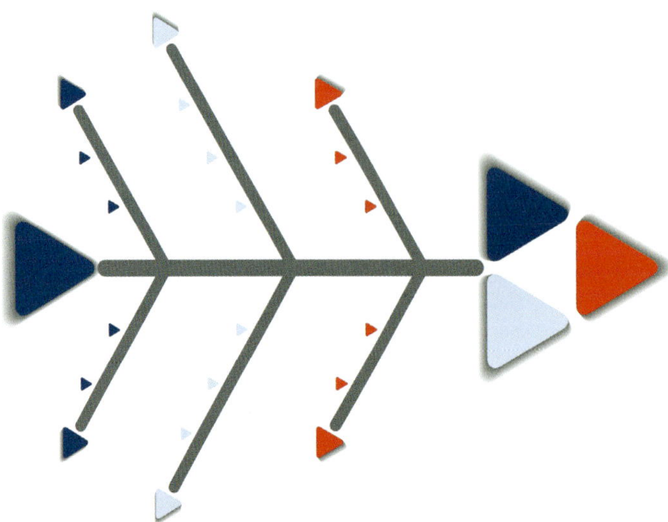



ISBN: 9780170389327

# 5 International migration

International Migration Reports from the United Nations give data on migrant populations and highlight key facts. The following data comes from the 2015 International Migration Report.

| **International migrants worldwide** | |
|---|---|
| **Year** | **Millions** |
| 2000 | 173 |
| 2010 | 222 |
| 2015 | 244 |

| **In 2015 two-thirds (67 percent) of migrants lived in just 20 countries** | | | |
|---|---|---|---|
| **Number (m)** | **Country** | **Number (m)** | **Country** |
| 47 | USA | 6 | Italy |
| 12 | Germany | 5 | India |
| 12 | Russia | 5 | Ukraine |
| 10 | Saudi Arabia | 4 | Thailand |
| 9 | UK | 4 | Pakistan |
| 8 | United Arab Emirates | 4 | Kazakhstan |
| 8 | Canada | 3 | South Africa |
| 8 | France | 3 | Jordan |
| 7 | Australia | 3 | Turkey |
| 6 | Spain | 3 | Kuwait |

| **Regions they lived** | |
|---|---|
| **Place** | **Millions** |
| Europe | 76 |
| Asia | 75 |
| Northern America | 54 |
| Africa | 21 |
| Latin America and Caribbean | 9 |
| Oceania | 8 |

| **Top refugee-producing countries (2015)** | |
|---|---|
| Syria | 3.9 million |
| Afghanistan | 2.6 million |
| Somalia | 1.1 million |

| **Female migrants** | |
|---|---|
| 2000 | 49% |
| 2015 | 48% |
| More female migrants than male in Europe and Northern America. | |
| More male migrants than female in Africa and Asia. | |

| **Estimated number of refugees in top host countries** | |
|---|---|
| Total | 19.5 million |
| Turkey | 1.6 million |
| Pakistan | 1.5 million |
| Lebanon | 1.2 million |
| Iran | 1.0 million |

| **Median age of international migrants** | |
|---|---|
| 2000 | 38 years |
| 2015 | 39 years |
| Between 2000 and 2015, median age got lower in Asia, Latin America and the Caribbean, and Oceania. | |

| Positive net migration between 2000 and 2015 |
|---|
| Contributed to 42% of the population growth in Northern America |
| Contributed to 32% of the population growth in Oceania |
| Contributed unknown amount to population growth In Europe; population in Europe would have fallen without net migration |

Net migration = Number of immigrants minus number of emigrants

| Populations in diaspora (outside their countries) | |
|---|---|
| India | 16 million |
| Mexico | 12 million |
| Russia | 11 million |
| China | 10 million |
| Bangladesh | 7 million |
| Pakistan | 6 million |
| Ukraine | 6 million |

| Major area of origin of migrants |
|---|
| 104 million born in Asia |
| 62 million born in Europe |
| 37 million born in Latin America and the Caribbean |
| 34 million born in Africa |
| 4 million born in Northern America |
| 2 million born in Oceania |

| Remittances |
|---|
| Migrants from developing countries sent home an estimated US$436 billion in remittances. |
| This was far more than<br>• official development assistance<br>• foreign direct investment (except in China). |

Remittances = money sent to family in home country

### Possible problems for migrants

- Remain among the most vulnerable members of society.
- First to lose job in an economic downturn.
- Working for less pay, for longer hours, and in worse conditions than other workers.
- Human rights violations, abuse and discrimination, exploitation.
- Migration remains one of the few options for people, particularly young people, to find decent work, and escape poverty, persecution and violence.

### Possible benefits of migrants to countries

- Fill critical labour shortages.
- Create jobs as entrepreneurs.
- Contribute in terms of taxes.
- Be some of the most dynamic members of society.
- Forge new paths in science, medicine and technology.
- Enrich their host communities by promoting cultural diversity.



ISBN: 9780170389327

# SKILLS PRACTICE

1 **Getting an Overview** | Get a general idea of the data by answering the following.

a What word shows you this data does not include people who are migrants but are still inside their own countries?

b Why does the totals for where migrants live not quite match the total number of international migrants?

c Why does a report like this published in 2016 use data for 2015?

d Why is this data now out of date?

e Why, even though the data is out of date now, is it still helpful in providing a general overview?

f What word is used for the act of sending money?

g What does the word 'possible' in front of 'benefits' and 'problems' want you to realise?

h What is a median age and how is it different to an average age?

i What word is used for migrants being spread around the world outside their own countries?

j What does net migration mean and how is it different to migration?

2 **Explaining Why** | Explain why the way the data for refugees is better presented the way it is than if it had been put into pie graphs.

3 **Language** | Find the words that mean the following.

a Actions that break or act against.

b Financial help given to developing countries.

c Unfair treatment of different groups of people.

d Treating unfairly so you can benefit from their work.

e Serious lack of resources for proper existence.

f Cruel treatment over long period of time.

g Exposed to the possibility of harm.

h Person who identifies a need such as a business and fills it.

i Having different cultures.

j Putting money, time or effort in to get profit later.

4 **Being Relevant** | Say why this graph does not belong with (is not relevant to) the data in this unit.

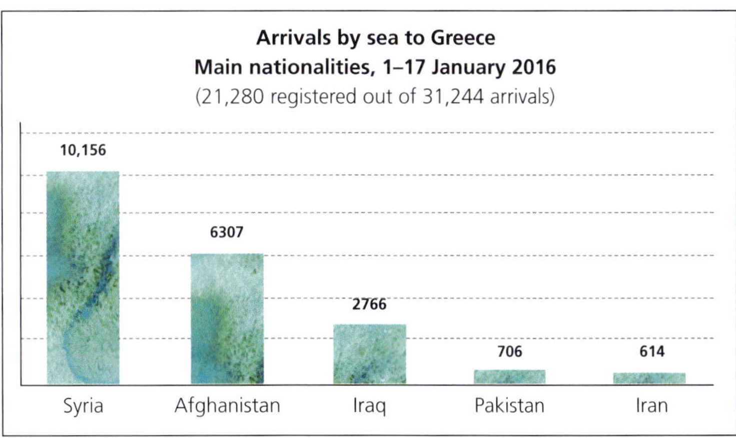


5 **Freehand Drawing** | Draw without digital help a bar graph to show numbers of international migrants by major area of origin in 2015.

ISBN: 9780170389327

# 6 Internal migration

With a population of about 1.4 billion in 2016, China was the most populous country in the world.

The biggest mass internal migration of human history is happening in China.

It is estimated that over the next 25 years, up to 345 million people will migrate in China.

Migration is mostly from central and western regions to eastern regions.

Migration is mostly from rural areas to urban areas.

Some experts call this migration the Second Industrial Revolution.

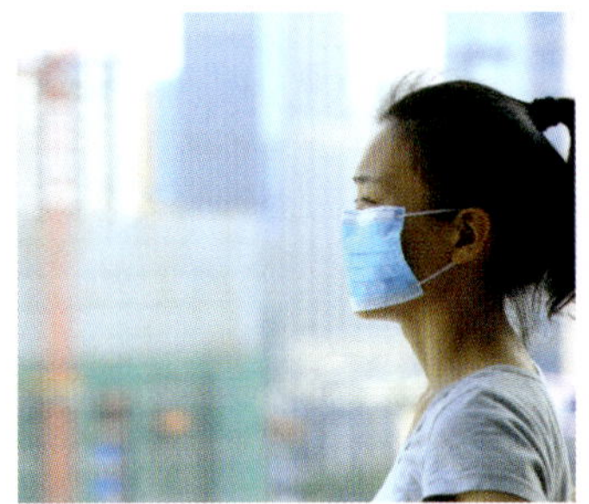

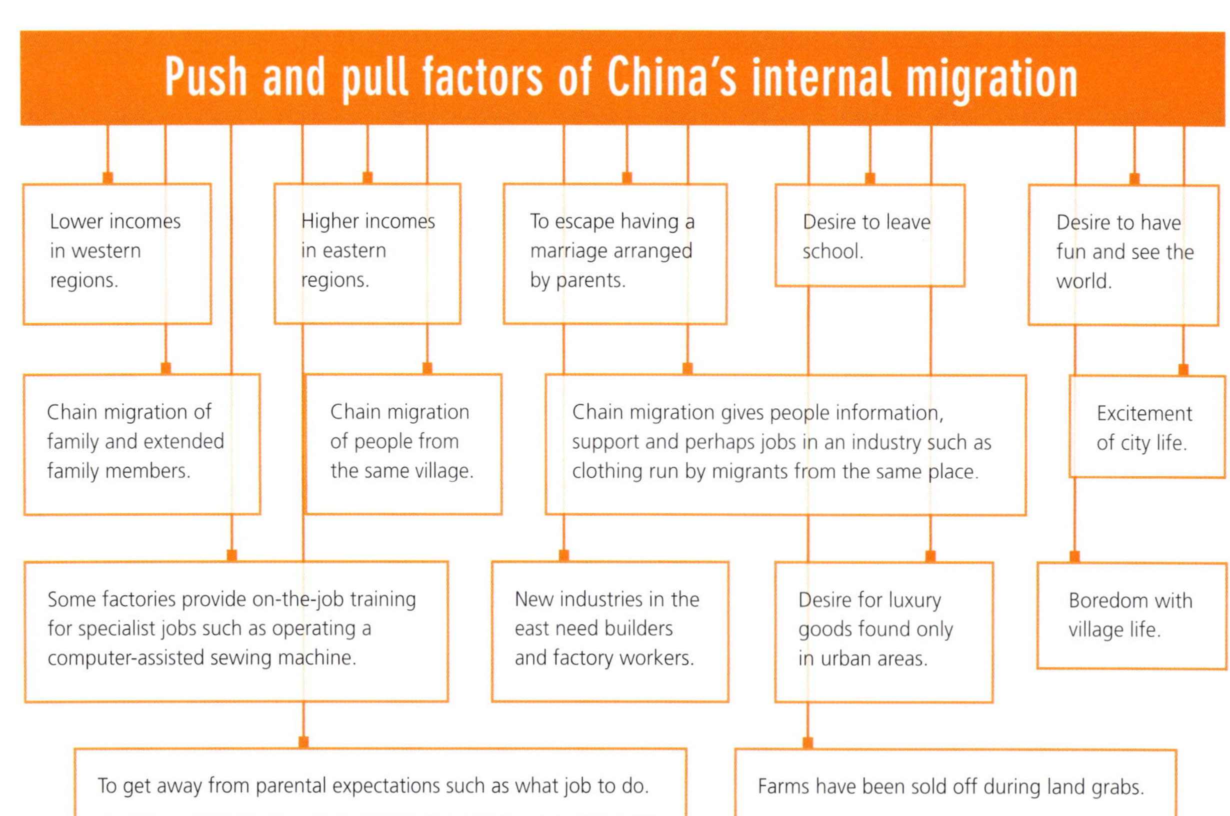




ISBN: 9780170389327

## Possible results of internal migration

| | |
|---|---|
| Skyrocketing urban population. | Migrants treated as lower-class citizens. |
| Migrants get jobs in transport, manufacturing, construction, household service (such as housekeeper, cook, masseur, cleaner, car washer). | Migrants known as 'floating population'. |
| Increased supply of labour in urban areas. | Children left behind with one parent, usually mother, or with grandparents. |
| Increased income for migrants. | Migrants work longer hours than what labour laws allow. |
| Access to different jobs for migrants. | Migrants work in dangerous jobs such as chemical factories and mines. |
| Remittances to families in rural regions. | Younger migrants especially can get involved in urban crime. |
| Migrant workers have higher standards of living. | Young males leave and remaining family less able to do heavy jobs. |
| Increase of new knowledge and skills for migrants. | Children have to work on farm rather than go to school. |
| Increased demand for services in urban regions. | Elderly relatives left behind in villages making ageing rural areas. |
| Increased pollution in urban regions. | Farms abandoned. |
| Overcrowding in areas of cities. | Not enough housing for all migrants. |
| Development of migrant suburbs with few services. | |
| Depopulation of rural regions. | |
| Increased demand for resources such as water in urban regions. | |
| China moves away from old agricultural culture. | |

## SKILLS PRACTICE

1 **Location** | Study the map of China and describe locations for the following places.

a The capital city (Beijing)
b The largest city (Shanghai)
c Hong Kong
d The capital of Tibet (Lhasa)
e The Yellow Sea
f The Pacific Ocean
g Taiwan
h Mongolia

2 **Relating Data To Cause and Effect** | State whether each source on page 22 is a cause OR an effect of internal migration and give a reason for each decision. Then supply a suitable caption for each source, making sure you include the word 'cause' or 'effect' in each caption.

**Source 1**

By 2012, China had a floating population of over 160 million people. A floating population consists of people in the area who do not live there permanently and are not in the official census count. China's floating population is mainly rural to urban migrants moving to the industrial centres of China's eastern seaboard.

**Source 2**

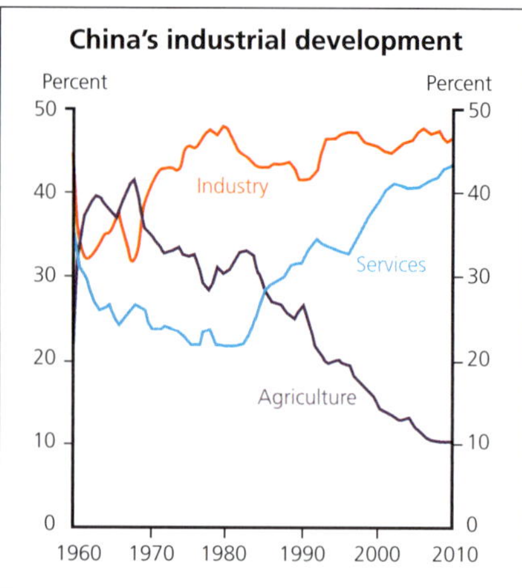


**Source 3**

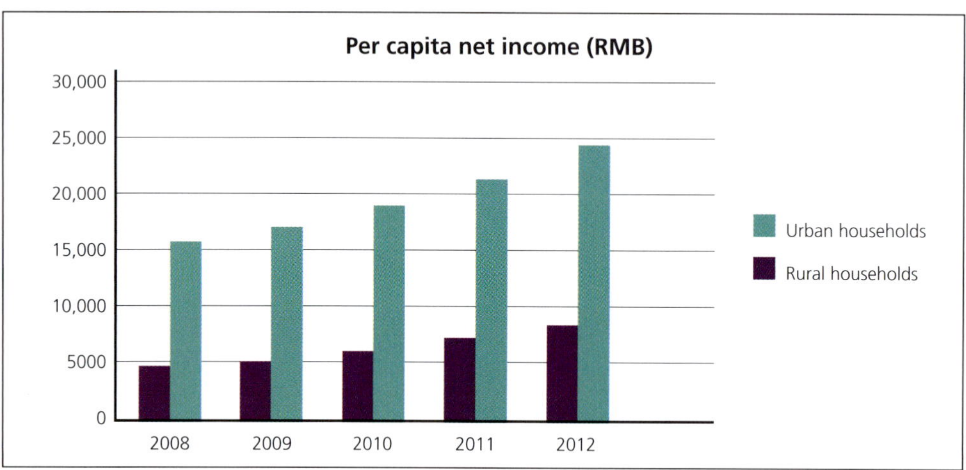


**3 Compare Two Countries** | Say how and why population movements in China and New Zealand are different.

**4 Graph Aim** | Explain the aim of this graph and how it achieves it.

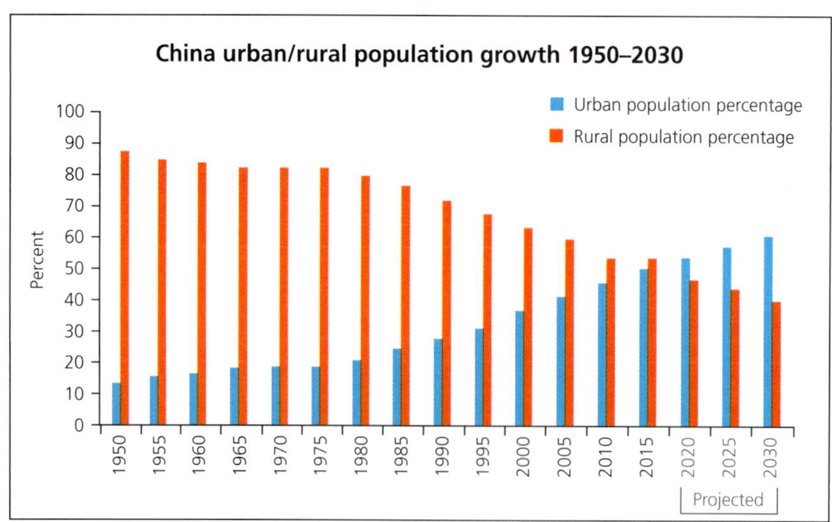


**5 Positive Versus Negative Impacts** | Separate the possible results of rural-urban migration into Positive Impacts and Negative Impacts.



 ISBN: 9780170389327

# 7 Child migrants

- A child is most usually defined internationally as someone under 18.
- Child migration is the movement of children within or across political borders, with or without parents or guardians, to another country or region.

Child migration is not new. From the 1920s to the 1960s, the UK sent 130,000–150,000 unaccompanied poor children to British colonies. Most went to Australia; 593 went to New Zealand. The aim was to give them better lives while they contributed a young British population to new places. Often, children were separated from siblings, told their parents were dead, abused, and made to do hard labour at farms and orphanages. In 2010 the British Prime Minister issued an apology for the 'shameful' and 'misguided' child resettlement programme and announced a fund to compensate affected families.

What is new is the scale of today's child migration. Organisations such as UNICEF (United Nations Children's Fund) write reports which gather global data about the migration of children and the effect it has on them. They know record numbers of migrant children arrive in Europe, but find it hard to get accurate numbers. As well as countries not always being helpful, many children don't want to give personal information to authorities in case they get returned to their country of origin.

## Some 2016 UNICEF data

- Children make up more than half the world's refugees, yet they are less than a third of the global population.
- About three-quarters of the world's child refugees come from just 10 countries.
- 45 percent of child refugees under the UNHCR are from Syria and Afghanistan.
- 50 million children have either migrated to another country or been forcibly displaced internally.
- Of these, 28 million children have been forced to flee by violence and conflict.
- 70 percent of children seeking asylum in Europe in 2016 were fleeing conflict in Syria, Afghanistan and Iraq.
- More and more children are crossing borders on their own.
- In 2015, over 100,000 unaccompanied minors applied for asylum in 78 countries — triple the number in the previous year.

## Push/Pull factors

- Conflicts and wars.
- Wanting a better, safer life.
- Extreme poverty.
- Violence in home.
- Violence in society.
- Drug trade gang violence.
- Parental wishes — parents in places such as Mexico and Guatemala, desperate for children to have a better life, send them off with human smugglers. They believe their children will get to stay with relatives in the USA, but that does not always happen.

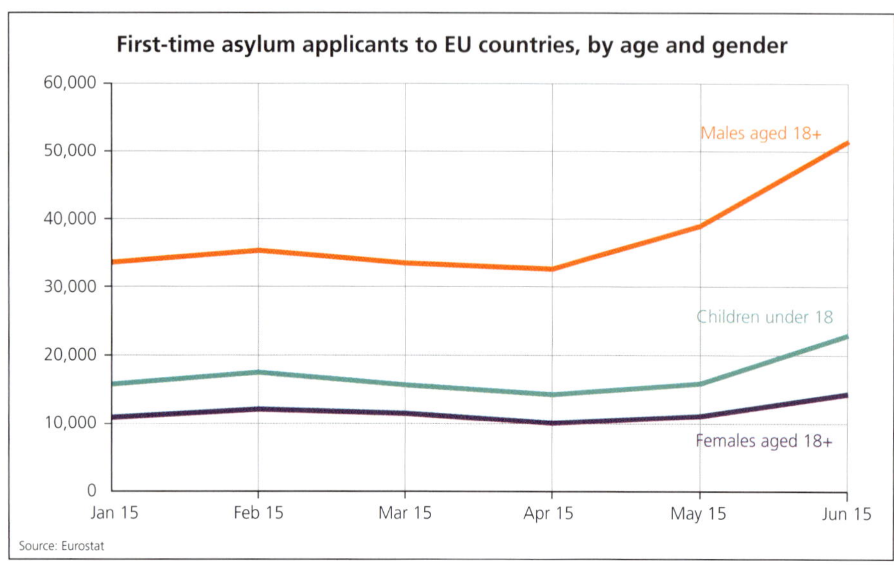


*This graph was produced before the UK voted in 2016 to leave the EU. In 2015 in the UK there were 3043 applications from unaccompanied asylum-seeking children, an increase of 56 percent since 2014.*

## Results of child migration

'Indelible images of individual children — Aylan Kurdi's small body washed up on a beach after drowning at sea or Omran Daqneesh's stunned and bloody face as he sat in an ambulance after his home was destroyed — have shocked the world,' said UNICEF Executive Director Anthony Lake. 'But each picture, each girl or boy, represents many millions of children in danger.'

1. Some child migrants are well-protected and cared for, migrate safely, and go on to live productive lives in new countries. Reports say that where there are safe and legal routes, migration can offer opportunities for both children who migrate and communities they join.
2. Many child migrants, already traumatised by the violence they fled, face all the dangers on migration that adults face, such as risk of drowning on sea crossings, lack of food and water, and lack of welcome.
3. Many get detained in camps because they have no documents.
4. There is no one system for tracking and monitoring them and thousands just disappear.
5. Data shows they are five times more likely to be out of school than non-migrants. Those who do go to school often face bullying.
6. Sometimes laws can stop them getting services in new countries.
7. Dislike from locals can escalate into physical attacks.
8. Babies are born every day along migration routes in bad conditions. Some are left at roadsides.
9. As families go along migration routes and through reception centres, get loaded on to buses and trains and then unloaded, it is easy for children to get lost.
10. Officials such as border guards and staff in reception and detention centres might not be sympathetic.
11. Children may clash with the law if they travel without documents, or if they steal to stay alive.
12. Adults might use children for illegal activities, such as images on the internet, child labour, drug trafficking or pick-pocketing.



ISBN: 9780170389327

# SKILLS PRACTICE

1 **Precis** | Make a précis (short summary of main points) of Child Migrants.

2 **Inaccurate Data** | The data on this map is from 2013 so it is well out of date. Suggest reasons that the data would not have been accurate at that time also.

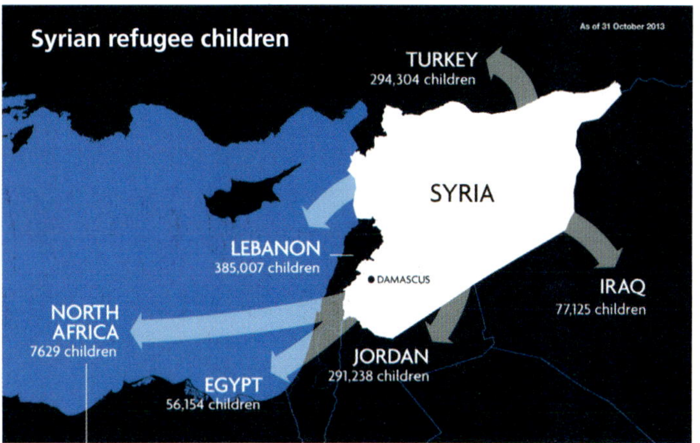


3 **Providing Examples** | Provide an example of 20th-century child migration and an example of 21st-century child migration and try to show some differences between them.

4 **Design** | Your task is to design an outline of something (for very young children it could be a teddy bear) into which data about child migrants can be put. Either describe how your design would look or present a finished product.

5 **Getting Essential Details** | Study the two sources below and answer the questions that follow.

Source 1

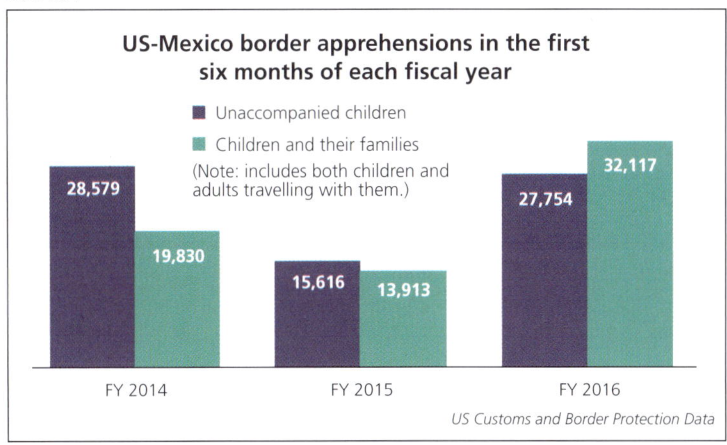


Source 2

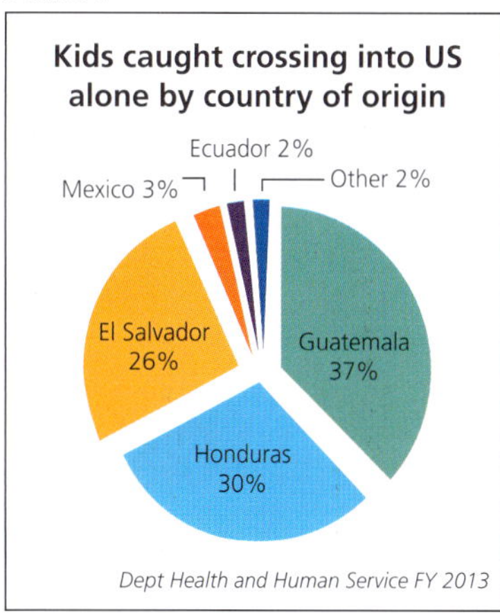


a Where did the data come from for Source 1?
b What does FY stand for and what is it telling you?
c What does 'apprehensions' mean?
d What does the use of 'apprehensions' suggest about the possibility of other people who do not figure in the data?
e What does the information in the 'Note' tell you?
f For what year is the data in the pie graph?
g What is the main aim of the pie graph?
h Why is it important to get the essential details of sources rather than making rushed judgements?

# 8 How a country produces migrants

Syria is located in the Middle East. Conflict that erupted in 2011 produced the worst human population crisis in the world. In 2011, pro-democracy protests led to violence which led to civil war as rebels fought Government forces. Other groups joined in, such as Isis (Islamic State) which took advantage of chaos to capture areas in Syria and Iraq, and then other countries got involved by giving support to some of the groups. Syria collapsed.

*This is Damascus, the capital of Syria, before 2011. It is the oldest continually inhabited city in the world. Until 2011 global travellers rated Syria one of the best places to visit.*

## RESULT = MASSIVE MIGRATION

By the beginning of 2016 the United Nations had identified:

- 6.6 million Syrians internally displaced within Syria and over 4.8 million Syrians as refugees outside Syria
- 95 percent of Syrian refugees hosted by just five countries (Turkey, Lebanon, Jordan, Iraq, Egypt)
- 2.7 million Syrian registered refugees in Turkey, many of whom lived in Government-run camps near the Syrian border
- over 1 million Syrian registered refugees in Lebanon, 53 percent of whom were children, living throughout the country as Lebanon chose not to set up refugee camps
- 628,427 registered Syrian refugees in Jordan although an earlier Jordanian census had shown 1.4 million Syrian refugees were in Jordan
- about one million had asked for asylum in Europe. The top host countries were Germany with over 300,000 Syrian refugees and Sweden with 100,000.



ISBN: 9780170389327

## Syrian population

- Because of the war, demographers had a difficult time trying to work out population statistics.
- Until 2011, they considered Syria a rapidly growing country in the region.
- In 2012, they estimated the population at 22.5 million. In 2016, they estimated the population at 18.2 million.
- The most populated city was Aleppo. They knew that Aleppo's population had dropped dramatically but not by how much.
- They thought that approximately 5000 fled Syria every day.
- The situation was further complicated because Syria had many refugees from other countries such as Iraqis and Palestinians.
- Syrian refugees placed pressure on host countries. A World Bank Report of 2016 showed Syrian refugees in Jordan had cost Jordan more than $2.5 billion a year, which was about a quarter of Government's annual revenues. This had swollen Jordan's public debt and badly damaged its economy. Most refugees in Jordan lived outside refugee camps, which added strain to infrastructure.

## The story of X

X was a young Syrian university student. If he had kept a diary of his migration, key points would have been the following.

Joined protests, now a wanted person by Government. War destroyed town, killed many in his family. Fled Syria for Europe.

Got into Libya, tried to sneak across border. Caught by guards, put in jail for few days. Went to Tripoli, worked for several months. Went to Zowara coastal city, made deal with people smuggler. Finally got on boat to Europe. Libyan coastguards stormed boat, detained for two days, let go. Found another people smuggler, got spot on next boat to Europe but smuggler kept lying about departure date while collecting more people. Finally got on boat, spent 30 hours without moving because overloaded. Egyptian rescue boat, back to Zowara. Got on another boat, overloaded, started to sink after few hours. Bailed water out with buckets. Helicopter circled for few minutes, left. Ship came, boat and ship hit, boat sank faster. Jumped off, swam for ship. Maltese coast guard and others took over five hours to rescue people; 39 dead.

Rescue boat dropped survivors in Sicily. Put in camp, to be fingerprinted next day. Escaped early morning, got up to Milan in Italy.

Headed to France, caught by French police, took fingerprints, sent back to Italy.

In Milan met smuggler, smuggled by car into Germany. Went to police, got refugee status three months later, became legal resident of Germany.

# SKILLS PRACTICE

1 **Geography |** Make a sketch copy, not a download, of the map showing the location of Syria. Learn the spelling of countries' names.

2 **Understanding a Story |** Refer to the story of X. Identify times his life was in danger and say why. Then say why X is an example of why statistics for migrant populations are approximate only.

3 **Using Photos |** Use these photos to help you prepare a short paragraph about how war has affected the population of Syria.

4 **Population Reading |** Explain how Syrian migrants affected population in Syria and other countries.

5 **Pieces of Information |** Find five pieces of information in this unit that could help explain the graph.

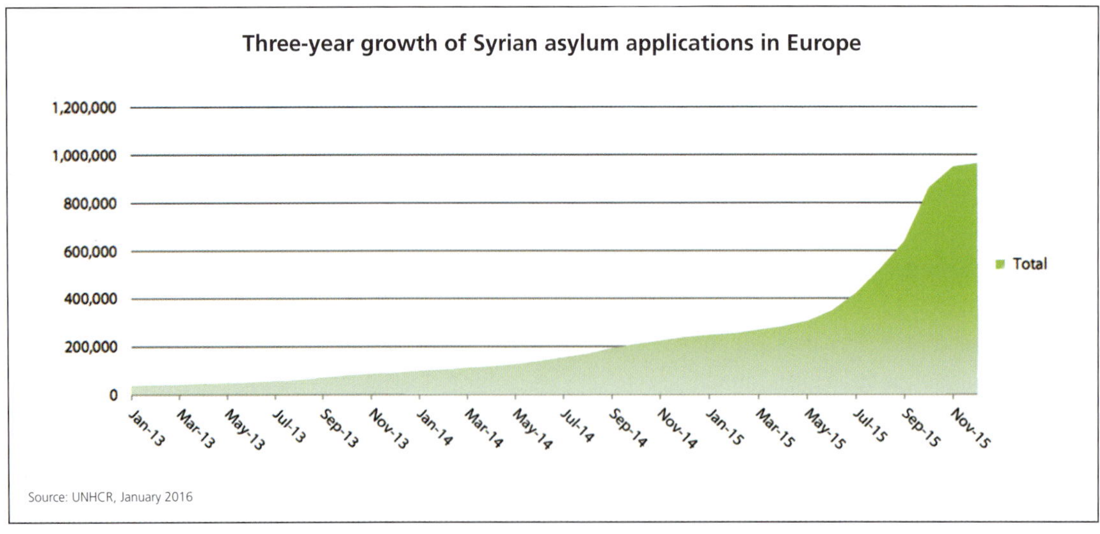




ISBN: 9780170389327

# 9 Illegal immigration

Countries have laws and rules about who can come in to live. They require immigrants to have documents such as passports and visas, which are certificates or stamps marked on a passport by immigration authorities. When they give people permission to come in, those people are legal migrants. When people come in without permission they enter illegally. Some are migrants who come in legally but do not leave when they should.

## Some opinions

'The world should stop using "illegal" to describe migrants. You can call the act illegal but you can't call people illegal. Better words would be undocumented, unauthorised or irregular.'

'We were fleeing poverty. I risked my life and the lives of my son and wife so they could have a nice life. They drowned when the migrant boat capsized. I wish I hadn't survived.'

'The better lives we get, even as illegals, are worth the risks of being caught and punished.'

'We shouldn't have borders between countries. People should be allowed to live in whatever country they want.'

'Article 13 of the Universal Declaration of Human Rights says everyone has the right to leave any country but it does not say that everyone has the right to enter any other country.'



'Population changes always have causes and results.'

## Impact of decreasing illegal labour in USA

Drug cartels operating on migrant routes into USA. Better border patrolling between USA and Mexico. High prices charged by human smugglers. USA upped numbers of illegal migrants it deports to hundreds of thousands each year.

While population of USA goes up, number of migrants unlawfully in USA stays steady at about 11 million.

Big impact on labour force where some areas such as agriculture, building and service industries have labour shortages.

ISBN: 9780170389327  

### New hotspot for illegal migration

With well over 80 million population, much poverty, and experts hoping it does not decline into chaos, Egypt had become the new hotspot for illegal migration launching through the Mediterranean to Europe.

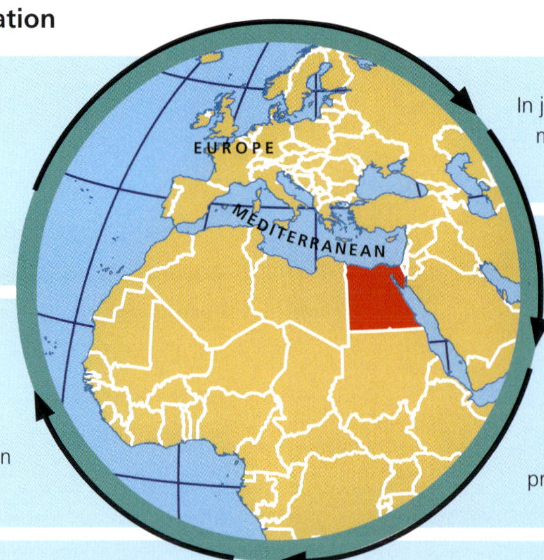


In just the first seven weeks of 2016, more than 84,000 illegal migrants reached the EU.

The Egyptian military said that besides rescuing 163 people from the capsized boat, border guards had stopped another illegal attempt by seizing a boat carrying 294 migrants on the Mediterranean Sea.

Experts warned the Mediterranean was becoming a mass grave. More than 2800 deaths were recorded between January and June of 2016, versus 1838 during the same period of the previous year.

In September 2016, world leaders, including the Egyptian President, had gathered in New York at the United Nations to discuss the migrant crisis when news came of a boat carrying about 600 Egyptian, Syrian and African migrants capsizing off Egypt. Survivors said the boat was kept off the coast for five days as more and more migrants were brought on board, and it capsized after a final group of about 150 were crammed in. Police detained many survivors and handcuffed the injured to their hospital beds.

## SKILLS PRACTICE

1 **Sharing Your Opinion** | Choose one of the opinions and write some sentences to show your own opinion on the issue.

2 **Thinking on Your Feet** | You were a world leader at the 2016 UN meeting about the migrant crisis. You were just about to deliver your prepared speech when you got news of the Egyptian boat disaster. What were your introductory remarks to the other world leaders?

3 **Reaction** | Explain how this migrant is contributing to population movements.

4 **Considering Factors** | List all the factors that make Egypt an important player in the story of illegal migration.

5 **Focusing Questions** | You are a journalist writing a piece about illegal immigration. Create five focusing questions that will help you gather information for your piece.



ISBN: 9780170389327

# 10 Migrant routes

The huge numbers of migrants trying to get into Europe brought images of the ancient sea 'in the middle of land', the Mediterranean, into homes around the world.

This is a route across Europe that many migrants fleeing from Syria took to reach Germany. By May 2016, it had become very hard to make the trip.

Fleeing through Syria to the Turkish border was just as dangerous as staying put. People moved at night to avoid snipers and soldiers; they found refuge in places such as old henhouses and sheds. Getting clean water and food was difficult.

Crossing the Turkish border meant dealing with human smugglers. The EU deal with Turkey said Turkey was to take back migrants who reached Greece via Turkey and to give temporary protection to Syrian returnees. Human rights groups reported Turkey deported Syrians back to Syria and deaths happened at the Syrian-Turkish border.

**Migrant routes**

SYRIA

Crossing the Mediterranean to Greece was a gamble. High winds, pelting rains and stormy seas could flip or sink rubber dinghies and overloaded boats. Rescue often came too late. Migrants also died from suffocation in holds or from inhaling poisonous fumes and survivors said smugglers charged money for letting people come out of the hold to breathe. Some boats ended up at overcrowded Greek islands rather than the mainland.

From then on there were closed borders to deal with. Macedonia closed its border to migrants, using tear gas, rubber bullets and stun guns to push them back from the border fence. Serbia closed its border to migrants and those stuck in a Macedonian camp tried to get over the border illegally at night. Some were caught and returned; others disappeared. Hungary closed its border and built a fenced topped with razor-wire and made it a criminal offence, punishable with deportation or prison, to damage the fence. At the Hungary-Austria border there were huge queues of traffic as the Austrian army searched every vehicle for migrants.

Once European and Turkish authorities started to crack down on boats from Turkey crossing to the Greek isles, many migrants began to use the illegal route through Libya and across the Mediterranean to Italy.

By about mid-2016, at least 235,000 migrants and refugees were on the coast of Libya waiting for a chance to cross the Mediterranean to Italy. By that time more than 128,000 migrants had reached Italy from North Africa.

Sicily had more than 6000 people land in just three days, as arrivals of migrants increased by 90 percent on the previous year.

The closest part of Italy to North Africa is a tiny island called Lampedusa. Coastguards take the wrecks of vessels on which migrants set out, to Lampedusa to finish rotting away.

The smugglers' system was to load their human cargo at midnight. They put some on inflatable boats with a bit of fuel and no crew, and some on to old fishing boats with a crew. They supplied a rescue number to call when migrants got out to international waters where boats would run out of fuel or start to sink. If migrants got lucky, Italian or Maltese coastguards or a legal vessel picked them up. Crews on illegal boats pretended to be migrants. Survivors got a ride to Italy where Red Cross people gave them a meal and a phone call to families.

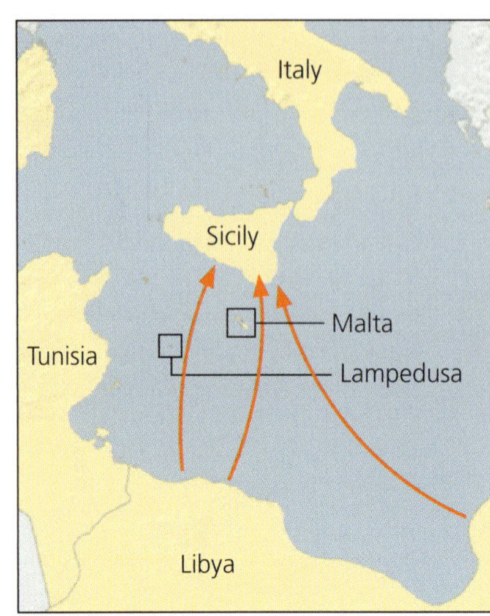


Some migrants ended up in the small country of Malta. The top countries from which migrants claiming asylum in Malta came were Libya, Syria, Eritrea and Somalia. They were mostly in refugee camps. In January 2016, a boat carrying about 122 migrants from Africa drifted in the sea for days. When it got to Maltese waters, about 35 people had died or disappeared. Maltese authorities rescued the 87 males found alive on board and put them in quarantine in Malta in case they were carrying diseases.

## SKILLS PRACTICE

1 **Looking Ahead** | You are a migrant who wants to get to Germany from Syria or from Libya to Italy. Choose which one and make a list of possible problems you will face. (The Mediterranean does have sharks.)

2 **Hypothesis** | Examine the graph and make a hypothesis (a reasoned guess that tries to explain something) about any pattern you see. Test your hypothesis by framing a question for the net and researching it. (Weather?)

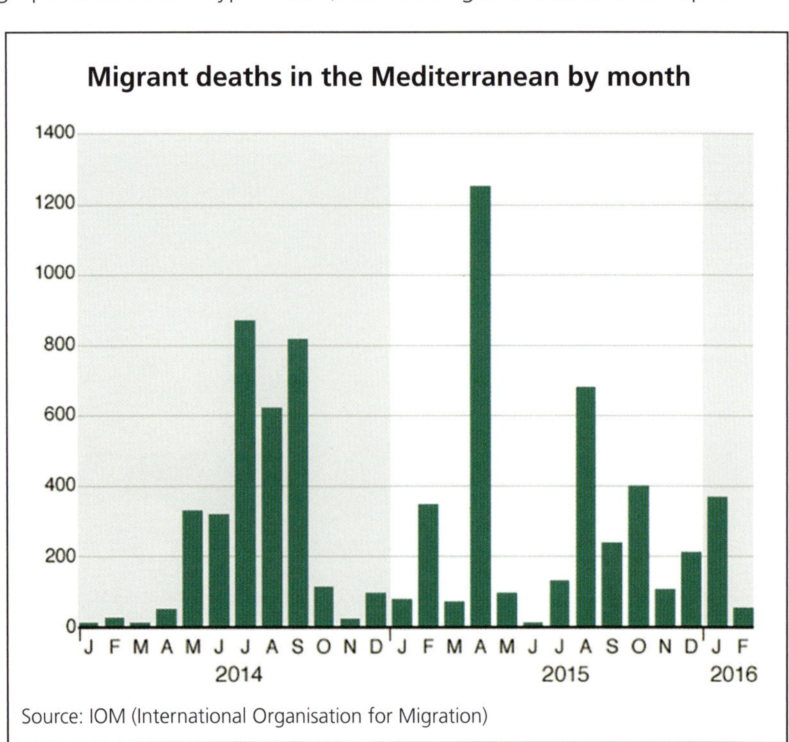


Source: IOM (International Organisation for Migration)



ISBN: 9780170389327

3 **Naming Mediterranean Locations** | Name the locations which best fit the following descriptions.

- **a** Housing rotting and wrecked migrant vessels.
- **b** Their coastguards rescue drowning and dying North African migrants.
- **c** Small island Mediterranean nation receiving African asylum seekers.
- **d** Libya's Mediterranean northwest neighbour.
- **e** First receiving country for migrants crossing Mediterranean from Turkey.
- **f** Reportedly deported migrants back to Syria.
- **g** Made deal with EU about migrants.

4 **Assessing Need** | Assess (decide) what the following needed to improve things for them.

- **a** Libya.
- **b** Red Cross workers.
- **c** Migrants rescued from Mediterranean.
- **d** Maltese coastguards.

5 **Photo Analysis** | Describe all the things you can observe in the photo. Describe all the things you can infer (make an informed guess) from the photo.

# 11 People smuggling

People smugglers deal in human cargo. Their aim is to make money from migrants whom they regard as goods to be moved like drugs and guns. As border controls between countries improve, migrants have two choices — try to cross borders illegally by themselves, or pay money to people smugglers to get them across. By the time migrants realise things are going wrong, it is too late to turn back.

One day Austrian police found an abandoned truck that was meant to be carrying frozen chickens. Inside the refrigerated lining with no air vents were 71 human corpses. A day later a truck in a small town close to the German border was stopped. Crammed inside, in a critical condition, were over 20 migrants from Syria, Afghanistan and Bangladesh. They were taken to hospital and their 29-year-old driver from Romania was arrested.

Some human smugglers have gained special reputations. Snakehead gangs in China smuggle workers into Western countries such as those in Western Europe, North America and Australia, and into some closer countries such as Japan and Taiwan. Coyote gangs smuggle people in to the USA.

**Official words from the United Nations**

Smuggling of migrants is the 'procurement, in order to obtain, directly or indirectly, a financial or other material benefit, of the illegal entry of a person into a State Party of which the person is not a national or a permanent resident.' (Article 3, Smuggling of Migrants Protocol)

States are to criminalise both smuggling of migrants and enabling of a person to remain in a country illegally. (Article 6 of the Smuggling of Migrants Protocol)

Europol says smuggling migrants is the fastest-growing criminal market in regions such as Europe. Smugglers can charge huge amounts of money. For example, migrants from East Africa might be smuggled along land routes to South Africa and then flown to Brazil. They then might be flown to Mexico rather than travel by sea or land. From there they are smuggled across the border in trucks, or on foot or train, or through tunnels. One Syrian-Palestinian refugee, an example of a migrant making money from other migrants, said he earned over two million dollars in six months by smuggling people across the Mediterranean from Egypt.



ISBN: 9780170389327

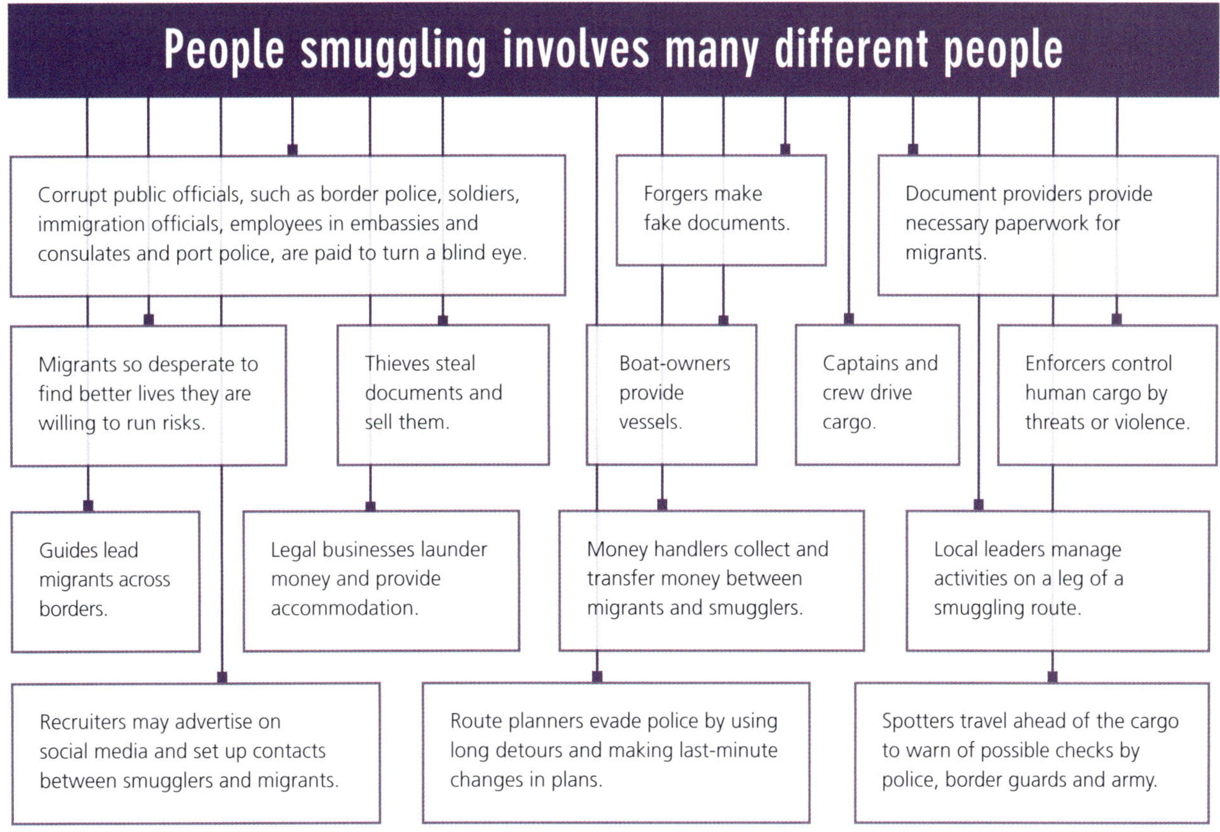


## SKILLS PRACTICE

1 **Linking** | Explain how each of the following is linked to people smuggling.

- **a** Snakeheads.
- **b** Planes.
- **c** Europol.
- **d** Coyotes.
- **e** United Nations.
- **f** Criminal migrant.

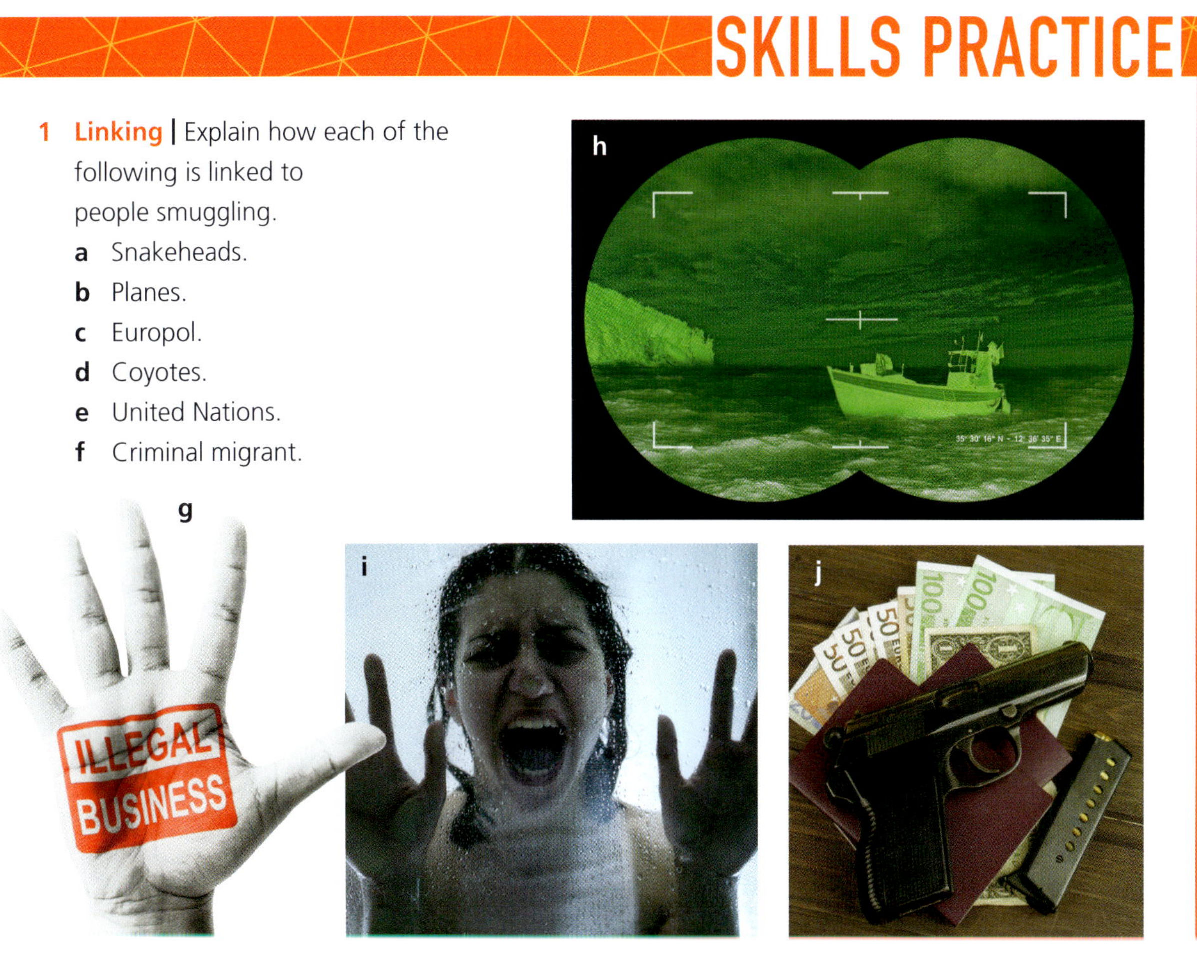

2 **Puzzle** | Make some notes about the following that you could use in a discussion about it.
*If one of the smuggled migrants gets a discount and is given the key to drive the lorry or the boat, is he or she a smuggler?*

3 **Haves and Have-nots** | Make a sketch copy of the map. Beside Europe put features that it has that the countries contributing migrants do not have.

**Major refugee routes to Europe**

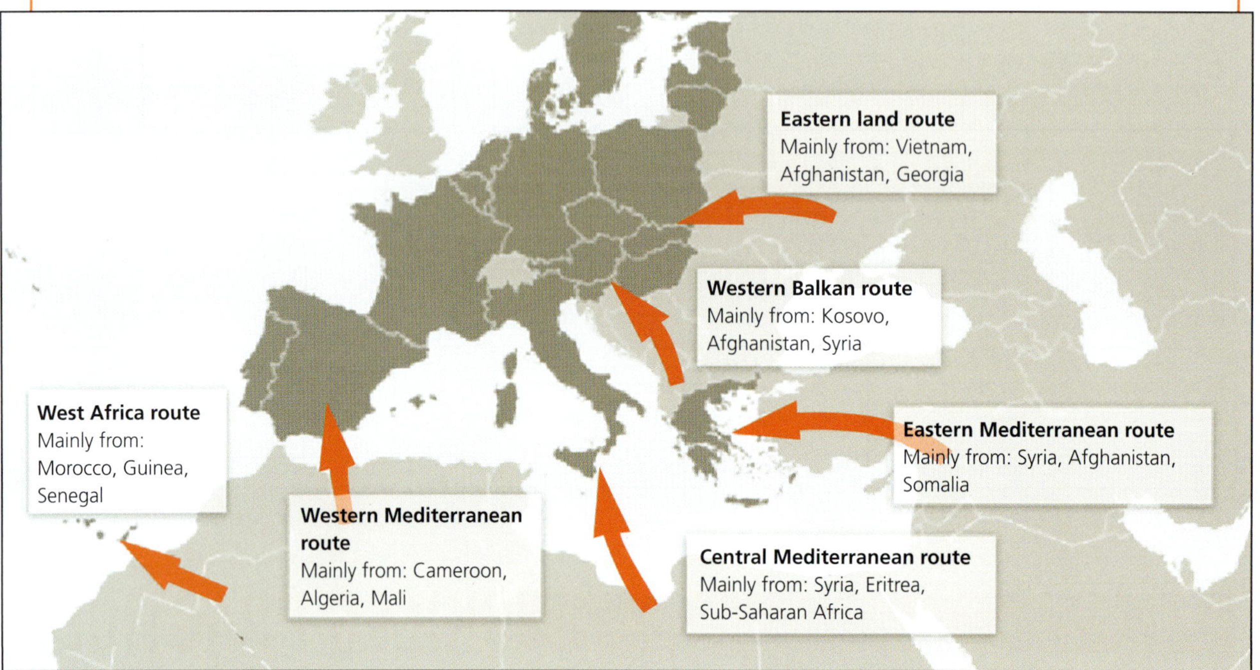


4 **Compiling** | Compile (produce by collecting data from sources) a list of people doing jobs for the smuggling process with brief job descriptions.

5 **Officialese** | Rewrite the definitions from the United Nations into everyday language.

ISBN: 9780170389327

# 12 Human trafficking

**Official definition of human trafficking**

'… the recruitment, transportation, transfer, harbouring or receipt of persons, by means of the threat or use of force or other forms of coercion, of abduction, of fraud, of deception, of the abuse of power or of a position of vulnerability or of the giving or receiving of payments or benefits to achieve the consent of a person having control over another person, for the purpose of exploitation. Exploitation shall include, at a minimum, the exploitation of the prostitution of others or other forms of sexual exploitation, forced labour or services, slavery or practices similar to slavery, servitude or the removal of organs.' (United Nations)

**Unofficial definition of human trafficking**

Human traffickers capture men, women and children by means such as snatching them from a street or by making false promises such as helping them to escape from their lives of poverty, and then forcing them into jobs such as hard labour, clothing factory work, sex slavery, forced marriage, begging, warfare, and supplying body parts.

## Differences between human trafficking and migrant smuggling

1 Migrants give consent. Trafficking victims don't consent, or if they are fooled into giving it the consent means nothing because the trafficker does not keep to the deal.
2 Smuggling ends with migrant delivered or abandoned; trafficking involves ongoing exploitation.
3 Smuggling involves crossing borders of countries; trafficking may not.
4 Smuggling is a crime against a country; trafficking is a crime against a person.

## What human trafficking and migrant smuggling have in common

- Routes.
- Methods of transport.
- Huge profits.
- Using human misery to make money.

## Results of trafficking

- Abuse of human rights.
- Removal of people from families and communities.
- Loss of human resources from countries of origin.
- Adding to criminals in many countries.
- Largely hidden crime. No accurate statistics kept about it.
- Goods made by trafficking victims are bought by consumers who don't know they are helping trafficking.
- Affects every country, as countries of origin, transit or destination.

In 2004 the US Government identified New Zealand as a destination for human trafficking. In 2016 NZ had its first conviction for human trafficking with a Fijian man called Ali found guilty of getting 15 Fijian workers to NZ on false promises of weekly wages of $900 for picking fruit. He charged huge fees for transporting them and many borrowed from family and friends. He then forced them to work illegally and live in overcrowded conditions while he underpaid them. It took almost 6000 man hours to gather enough evidence against Ali to start a prosecution.

ISBN: 9780170389327

## SKILLS PRACTICE

1 **Analysing a Formal Document** | Answer the following about the official definition of human trafficking.

- **a** Which international group is responsible for the definition?
- **b** How does it compare with the unofficial definition and why?
- **c** Quote the words that are about the act — what is done.
- **d** Quote the words that are about the means — how it is done.
- **e** Quote the words that are about the purpose — why it is done.
- **f** Supply the words that mean the following:
  - **i** getting new people
  - **ii** promise to provide work to repay money
  - **iii** sheltering
  - **iv** use force or threats to persuade
  - **v** fooling and deceiving
  - **vi** taking people away against their will
  - **vii** able to be easily hurt
  - **viii** criminal deception for gain
  - **ix** made to
  - **x** treating badly to profit from their work

2 **Venn Diagram** | Draw a large Venn diagram to show differences and similarities between human trafficking and human smuggling.



ISBN: 9780170389327

**3 Pictogram** | Describe what is happening in this pictogram.

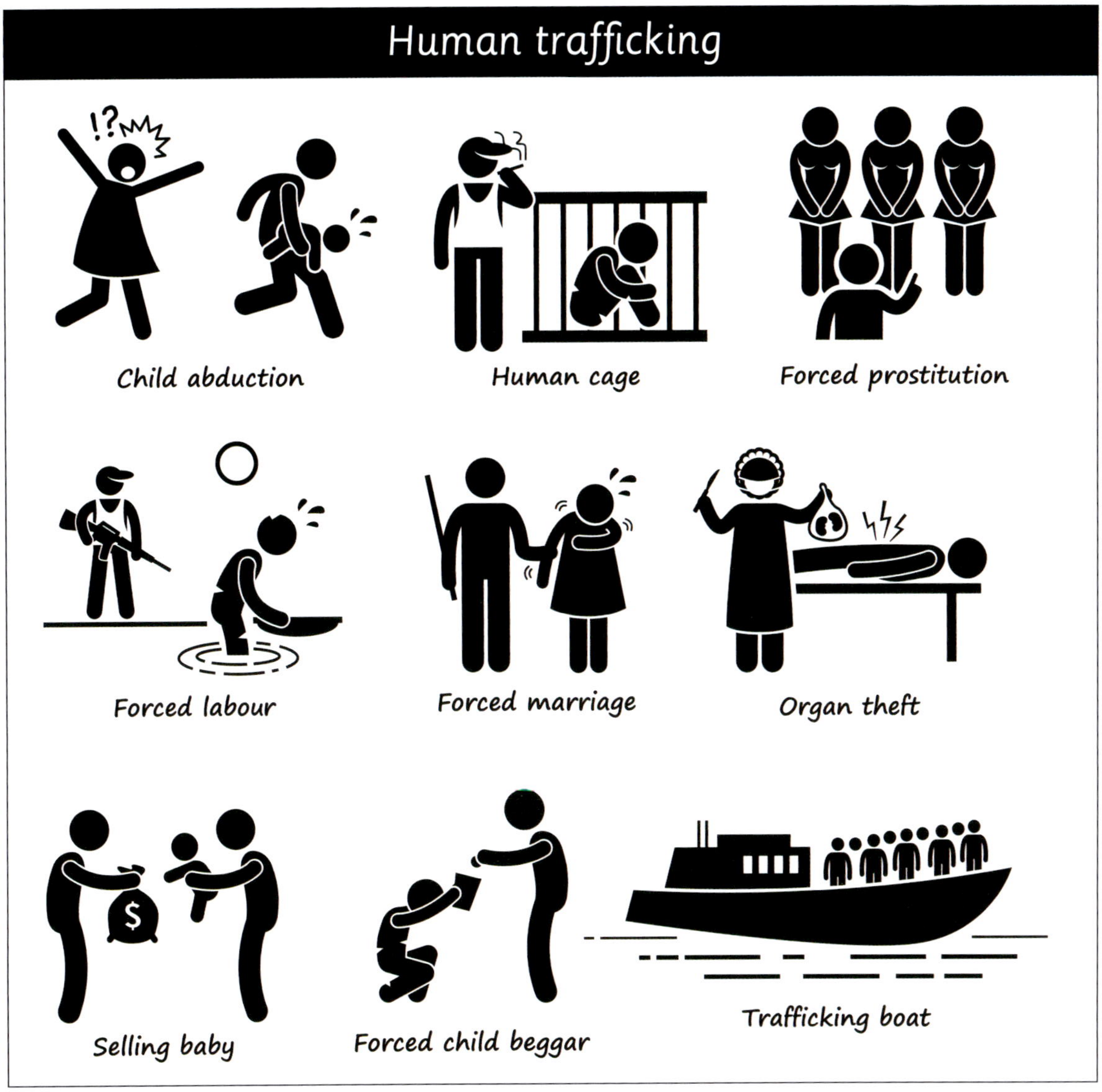
Human trafficking
Child abduction
Human cage
Forced prostitution
Forced labour
Forced marriage
Organ theft
Selling baby
Forced child beggar
Trafficking boat

**4 Speech-writing** | You are representing New Zealand at a Model United Nations. Write a short speech about why the world should pay more attention to human trafficking.

STOP
HUMAN
TRAFFICKING

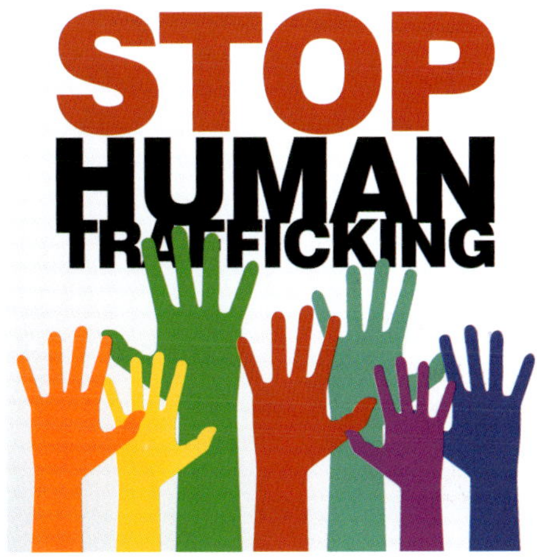

**5 Profiling** | Create a profile, a list of likely characteristics, motives and behaviours, for a human trafficker. For example, you have already seen that the trafficker is not always male. Think of the trafficker's impact on the victim.

# 13 Unplanned population explosion

From about 1999, migrants started to arrive in the Calais Jungle, the nickname for a makeshift camp they set up on wasteland in Calais, France. They aimed to get to the UK by stowing away on lorries, ferries, cars, or trains. Most were young males and did not speak French. Many had paid smugglers to get them to Calais.

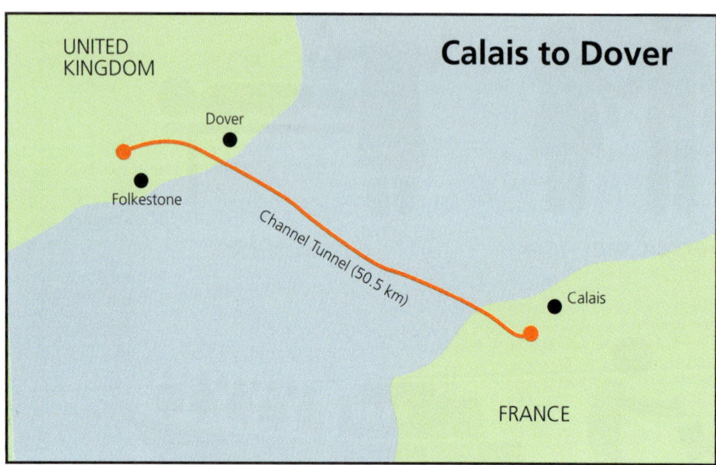


| Calais Jungle migrants | |
|---|---|
| Afghani | 36% |
| Sudanese | 32% |
| Pakistani | 8% |
| Eritrean | 8% |
| Ethiopian | 5% |
| Iraqi Kurds | 3% |
| Syrian | 3% |
| Irani | 2% |
| Kuwaiti | 2% |
| Others | 1% |

## Results of an exploding migrant population at Calais

The UK blamed France for not doing enough to stop migrants from getting into the tunnel, climbing fences along the border, stowing away in vehicles and disrupting train services. It supplied security fencing for the Eurotunnel where vehicles are loaded on to train shuttles. The port was protected by five-metre fences topped with coils of razor wire and CCTV with gates and armed French riot police as guards.

French authorities were faced with the problem of looking after migrants without attracting more of them.

When charity groups asked migrants what they needed, migrants said, 'Open the border.'

Hundreds of shopkeepers and restaurant owners from Calais held a protest in Paris to complain that the migrants had caused them to suffer heavy financial losses.

In March 2016, French authorities evicted migrants in the southern part of the camp and brought bulldozers in to clear it. Some migrants set fire to tents in protest and riot police used tear gas against stone-throwers. Some migrants sewed their mouths shut in protest. Evicted migrants went to other camps such as Dunkirk, camped out in cliff caves, or went into the northern sector of the Jungle.

The Hungarian Prime Minister, who was critical of Germany's open-door policy for migrants, said the EU should set up a giant refugee city on the Libyan coast and process asylum claims from those arriving from Africa.

In September 2016 the French President said he would shut down the Calais Jungle within weeks and send 9000 migrants to reception centres across France. Those who qualified for asylum could stay in France; he would deport the rest. Opponents said they would refuse to receive Calais migrants and said the plan would result in a host of mini-Calais across France.



ISBN: 9780170389327

# SKILLS PRACTICE

1 **Sketch from Aerial Photo** | Make a sketch from this aerial photo. Describe the main features the photographer would have been looking at.

2 **Describing and Assigning Actions** | Describe what the following actions are and who was most likely to do them.

- **a** Stow away.
- **b** Build rough shelters.
- **c** Annoy France.
- **d** Annoy the UK.
- **e** Deport.
- **f** Throw stones.
- **g** Protest against the Jungle.
- **h** Sew mouths shut.
- **i** Guard the port.
- **j** Risk their lives.
- **k** Disrupt train schedules.
- **l** Ask for open borders.

3 **Population Explosion** | Explain the factors that caused the Calais camp to be located where it was and to cause a mini population explosion there. (Clue = The French authorities did not plan it.)

4 **Population Numbers** | Use logic to match the numbers in the box to the following.

- **a** Population before camp was closed.
- **b** Unaccompanied children in the camp.
- **c** Left before the October eviction.
- **d** New centres in France built to house removed migrants.
- **e** Police needed to close the camp and move migrants.

| 450 |
|---|
| 1200 |
| 1000 |
| 10,000 |
| 20 percent |

5 **Follow Up** | Find out how the camp population was cleared and what happened to the migrants.

ISBN: 9780170389327

# 14 Problem-solving with slaves

*Armed slavers march slaves from African interior.*

*Plan of lower deck of boat with stowage of 292 slaves.*

GEOGRAPHY LOCATIONS TO KNOW

**The Old World** = what Europeans called Africa, Europe and Asia.

**The New World** = what Europeans called the Americas.

**Caribbean** = Caribbean Sea and its islands to the southeast of North America.

**The West Indies** = basically the same region as the Caribbean and often used to mean the same region.

**Virginia** = early British colony in North America.

*Slave auction in Virginia in 1856.*

## The problem

Several centuries ago, some countries in Europe, such as Britain and France, started to build empires by taking over areas in places such as the Americas and turning them into colonies. They wanted to use the colonies to make money, such as setting up sugar cane plantations. They needed workers for this but the arrival of Europeans in the Americas had brought diseases that killed many locals, and besides, paid labour cost a lot of money. So they turned to Africans who were excellent workers, were used to a tropical climate and tropical diseases, and were agricultural experts. But how to get Africans to leave their homes in Africa and go to the Americas?

## The solution

They set up a slave trade to kidnap Africans, ship them to the Americas, and sell them to plantation owners. Slave traders raided villages and captured people. Some African societies had their own slaves and were willing to sell slaves to slave traders. This slave trade was forced migration because slaves had no say. The system operated from the late 16th century to the early 19th century.

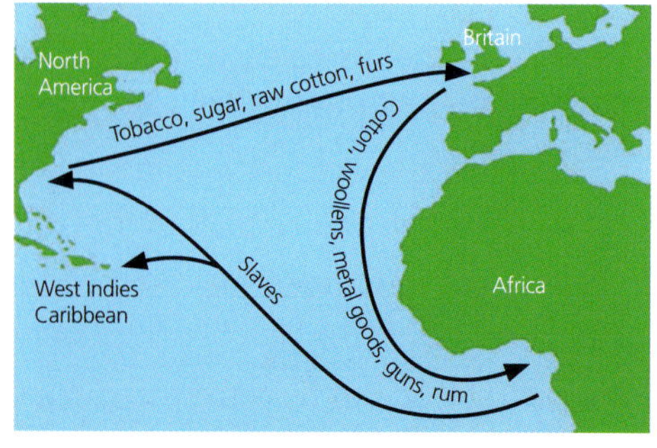




ISBN: 9780170389327

# Destinations of African slaves

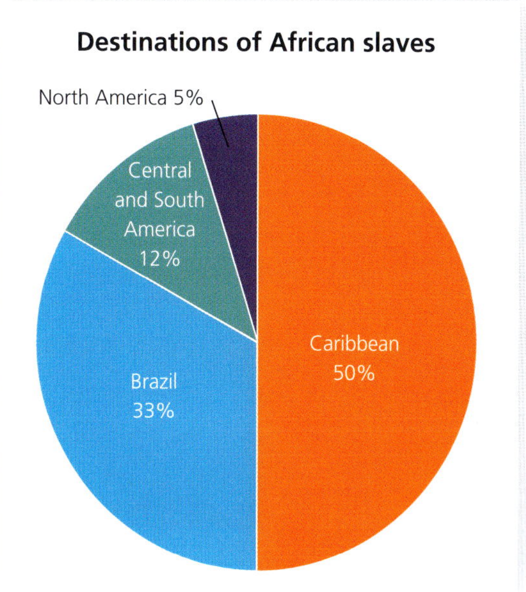


**Results**

1. Because few records were kept, nobody knows for certain how many Africans became human cargo for slavers. Most modern historians say 9–11 million, although some say it was higher.
2. Many slaves died on the forced march from their homes to the coast. Many died in buildings called slave forts as they waited for slave ships to collect them. Many died on board slave ships. Many died in the New World from overwork, slave revolts and diseases new to them.
3. It is thought that about two-thirds of the slaves taken to the New World were male. This affected the ratio of sexes in communities from where slaves were taken.

One record does refer to slave deaths at the West African coast. Business papers of British slave trader James Rogers have been preserved. They show that out of 939 slaves bought for Rogers during 1790, 203 died before they were put on board ship.

4. In the New World the slave trade made a division between rich white communities and poor black communities.
5. It reduced population in West Africa, especially along the coast.
6. European countries used the resources of Africa — people as slaves — for several hundred years.
7. The Rastafari movement in Jamaica, where a large percentage of the people are descended from slaves, has publicised slavery through reggae music.
8. The United Nations has set 23 August as the International Day for the Remembrance of the Slave Trade and its Abolition (getting rid of it).
9. Some apologies for the slave trade have been made. Examples are the President of Benin and the President of Ghana apologising for the role Africans played in the slave trade, the Liverpool City Council and the Mayor of London apologising for their city's part in the slave trade, and Virginia being the first US state to acknowledge its involvement in it.
10. It divided public opinion about values.

# The *Zong* affair

**Source 1**

On 6 September 1781 the slave ship *Zong* left the west coast of Africa for Jamaica with about 470 slaves. As slaves were valuable cargo, the captain had overloaded the ship. The owners had taken out insurance on the lives of the slaves as cargo. Dead slaves would earn the ship-owners nothing. During the voyage, supplies of drinking water ran low and the crew threw about 133 slaves overboard to drown, meaning the slaves were officially lost at sea and insurance would cover the loss. The crew claimed that by getting rid of some slaves, it would save the others. After the *Zong* reached Jamaica, the owners made a claim to their insurers for the loss of slave cargo. The matter went to court to decide if the insurance company should pay out.

ISBN: 9780170389327

**Source 2**

*An engraving from 1782.*

**Source 3**

'What is this claim that human people have been thrown overboard? This is a case of chattels or goods. Blacks are goods and property; it is madness to accuse these well-serving honourable men of murder. They acted out of necessity and in the most appropriate manner for the cause. The late Captain Collingwood acted in the interest of his ship to protect the safety of his crew. To question the judgement of an experienced well-travelled captain held in the highest regard is one of folly, especially when talking of slaves. The case is the same as if wood had been thrown overboard.' (Great Britain's Solicitor General at a trial)

## SKILLS PRACTICE

1 **Converting Text into a Cycle** | Read the description of the trade system below and draw a labelled diagram to show the cycle.

> Ships from Europe took manufactured goods to West Africa. The goods were used to buy slaves from traders. Ships took slaves to the New World where they were sold to sugar planters. Money from the sale bought sugar. Ships took sugar to Europe where it was sold. Money from the sale bought manufactured goods.

2 **Primary and Secondary Sources** | Study the *Zong* affair and decide which of the three sources are primary sources (created at or about the same time as the event) and which are secondary sources (created later by people who were not eyewitnesses and know about the event only because of the primary sources). Give reasons for your decision.

3 **Finding Proof** | Use the pie graph of Destinations of African Slaves to prove whether or not the following are accurate statements.

> Far more slaves were taken to South America than to the north.

> Fewer slaves were taken to the Caribbean than to the north.

4 **Bias** | Bias is showing a liking or dislike, especially in a way thought to be unfair. Choose two images in this unit. For your first image, prepare a few sentences describing what is happening from the point of view of someone against the slave trade. For your second image, prepare a few sentences describing what is happening from the point of view of someone in favour of the slave trade.

5 **Values Judgement** | Should countries who were involved in the slave trade issue formal apologies? (Some people say countries are too scared to do so because they fear having to pay compensation.) Make notes about your ideas on this issue.



ISBN: 9780170389327

# 15 White slave cargo

**Slavery was not just Europeans turning Africans into human cargo. Africans also forced Europeans to become human cargo.**

The Barbary Coast was what Europeans from the 16th to the 19th century called the Mediterranean coastline of North Africa. Among the population there was a group known as the Barbary pirates. They were mainly Muslim, although some had other religions and might even have come from Europe.

Atlantic Ocean
Europe
Mediterranean Sea
Salé
Rabat
Algiers
Tunis
Tripoli
BARBARY COAST
Africa

The pirates operated out of the ports of Salé and Rabat (in today's Morocco), Algiers (in today's Algeria), Tunis (in today's Tunisia), and Tripoli (in today's Libya).

Pirates kidnapped up to an estimated 1.25 million Europeans, mainly white Christians, and carried them back to North Africa. There they sold them as slaves in the slave markets along the coast.

Pirates targeted people on and around the Mediterranean Sea and the Atlantic Ocean. They attacked and seized thousands of ships, looting goods and kidnapping sailors. They landed on beaches and crept up on settlements in the dark to capture inhabitants. Survivors abandoned their homes and fled.

Some slaves died on the forced migration to North Africa. Survivors were auctioned off at slave markets. Owners gave them jobs ranging from housework to quarrying and rowing galleys. Some galley slaves had to live on galleys for years in chains and were not allowed to leave their seats even to attend to bodily functions.

There is one record of a raid by Barbary pirates — in Ireland on 20 June 1631, at Baltimore village on the coast. Pirates attacked at night, captured some local Irish and over a hundred English settlers who worked for a pilchard industry in the village. Pirates put captives in irons and took them to North Africa as slaves. After the raid, the remaining people of Baltimore moved away.

## Impact of the Barbary pirates

*Sancho Panza and Don Quixote.*

1 Some Europeans had relatives willing and rich enough to pay a ransom to free them. Miguel de Cervantes, a Spaniard who wrote a famous book about Don Quixote and his offsider Sancho Panza, was serving as a soldier when pirates captured him and took him to Algiers where they kept him as a slave from 1575 to 1580 until his parents paid a ransom.
2 A few of those who were ransomed made money by selling their stories but most found it hard to settle down and their communities sometimes were suspicious of them.
3 Some of those who 'turned Turk' (slang for converted to Islam) to avoid slavery in North Africa could not cope with the different culture and died, while others acclimatised to life in North Africa and some became important figures in society, which they would not have been able to do in their home countries.
4 Other slaves lived shortened lives as property of North African masters.

## SKILLS PRACTICE

1 **Improving a Map** | Make your own copy of the Barbary Coast map and improve it by adding features such as a title, symbols (maybe pirate ships) and a key/legend.

2 **Finding Differences** | Explain the differences between the two things in each of the following.
- **a** Voluntary and involuntary migration.
- **b** Working in quarries and rowing galley ships.
- **c** Looting and kidnapping.
- **d** Christian and Muslim.
- **e** Miguel de Cervantes and Don Quixote.
- **f** 'Turning Turk' and remaining Christian.

3 **Matching** | The following are answers to questions; what might have been the questions?

| | | | |
|---|---|---|---|
| **a** pirates | **b** fish | **c** Mediterranean | **d** auction |
| **e** Muslim | **f** ransom | **g** Libya | **h** galley |

4 **Providing Evidence** | Provide evidence that backs up the following statements.
- **a** Slavery was not something that only white people did to black people.
- **b** The raid on Baltimore made survivors feel unsafe.
- **c** The Barbary pirates treated kidnapped Europeans as cargo.
- **d** 'Turning Turk' could be a good career move.
- **e** Galley slaves had a harsh life.
- **f** Culture shock can kill.

5 **Illustrating** | Tell the story of the Barbary pirates in 10 or fewer pictures. You don't have to draw the pictures; you could just say what you would get an artist to draw.



ISBN: 9780170389327

# 16 Indentured migrants

The word indenture comes from the Middle Ages. It was a legal contract written twice on one sheet of paper. The two copies were separated by cutting along a jagged, toothed line so that the indented teeth of the copies could later be fitted together to show they were not forged. Each party to the contract kept a copy.

Indentured migrants were people who signed indentured contracts to work for a set amount of time such as five or ten years.

**Cause**

The British system of indentured labour involving workers from India, which was ruled by Britain as part of the British Empire, began after Britain abolished slavery in its empire in 1833. In the British colonies, newly-freed men and women refused to work for the low wages on offer. This led to a shortage of labour.

**Event**

The solution was a system of indentured labour that lasted until the British Government abolished it in 1917. Labourers were recruited to work in British colonies, and colonies of other European countries, in places such as sugar cane fields, cotton and tea plantations, factories, rubber plantations and where railways were being built.

**Result**

By the time it ended, Britain had transported about three and a half million Indians to colonies. This caused population changes. For example, Fiji has a large population of Indians today.

## How the process worked

Recruitment agents went into Indian villages. Indians listened because agents offered an escape from famine and poverty. Some agents exaggerated the amount of money labourers would get. Some lied about places, saying labourers would go to cities like Calcutta, but once the Indians had signed contracts they were taken to a ship that set sail for a foreign country instead.

Many Indians could not read or write. They signed the indentured contract with a mark like an X or a thumbprint. It meant they had not understood the terms of the contract.

Labourers went before a magistrate to say it was their choice to migrate, and they were vetted to make sure they were healthy and fit before transportation. But ships were overcrowded and many Indians died.

In their new jobs, Indians were supposed to get wages, a bit of land and sometimes a return passage. Most often, working conditions were harsh, wages low, and working hours long. Children were expected to work alongside parents from the time they were five years old.

The death rate for workers in Jamaica in 1870 was 12 percent; 30 years later Mauritius had the same percentage. An estimated seven percent of the several thousand Indian indentured workers who built the Kenya-Uganda railway died during their contract. Man-eating lions also attacked, killing around a hundred workers.

Some workers tried to escape but were recaptured, flogged and imprisoned. Sometimes their five-year contract was doubled to ten years for attempted desertion.

At the end of the contract, some Indians chose to return home, and others decided to stay where they were.

## SKILLS PRACTICE

1 **Labelled Sketch** | Make a labelled sketch to show how the term 'indenture' came about.

2 **Untitled Map** | Work out how this map relates to Indian indentured labour and suggest a suitable title for it.

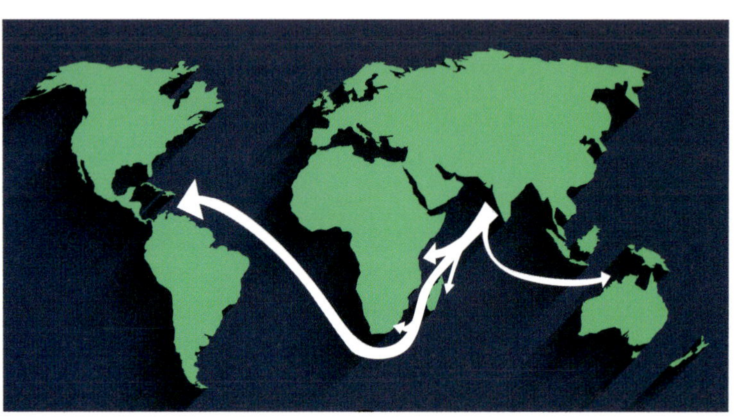

3 **Situations** | Name a situation you might have been up close and personal with for each of the following if you were an indentured Indian.

- **a** a man-eating lion
- **b** an unexpected destination
- **c** dead human cargo
- **d** a dishonest person
- **e** an X
- **f** a choice of to stay or go
- **g** a contract
- **h** a magistrate
- **i** a child worker
- **j** a doubling of years on a contract

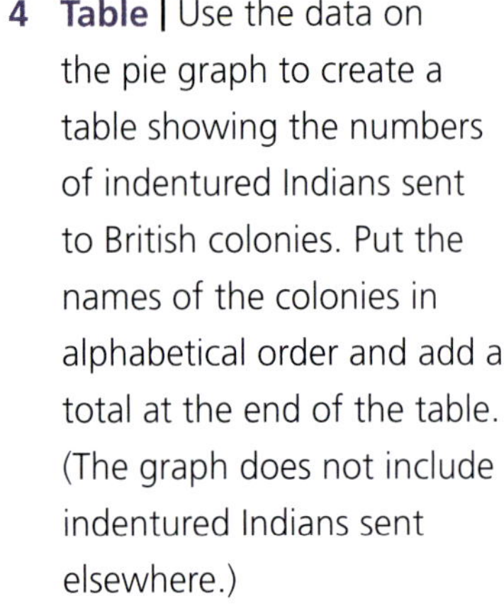

4 **Table** | Use the data on the pie graph to create a table showing the numbers of indentured Indians sent to British colonies. Put the names of the colonies in alphabetical order and add a total at the end of the table. (The graph does not include indentured Indians sent elsewhere.)

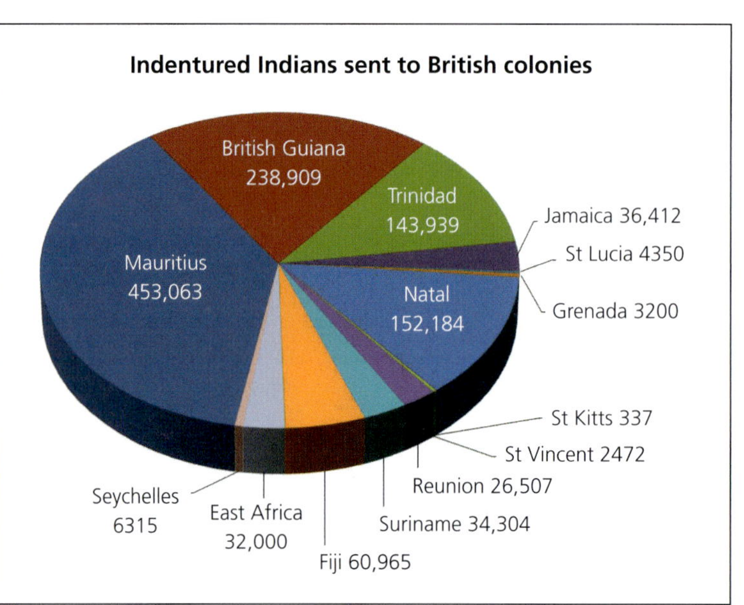




ISBN: 9780170389327

**5 Close Reading** | Read the following extracts from an Indenture Agreement of 1912 and answer the questions about them.

1 *Period of Service — Five Years from the Date of Arrival in the Colony.*

2 *Nature of labour — Work in connection with the Cultivation of the soil or the manufacture of the produce on any plantation.*

3 *Number of days on which the Emigrant is required to labour in each Week — Everyday, excepting Sundays and authorised holidays.*

9 *Conditions as to return passage — Emigrants may return to India at their own expense after completing five years' industrial residence in the Colony.*

11 *Other Conditions — Emigrants will receive rations from their employers during the first six months after their arrival on the plantation according to the scale prescribed by the government of Fiji ...*

13 *Suitable dwelling will be assigned to Emigrants under indenture free of rent and will be kept in good repair by the employers. When Emigrants under indenture are ill they will be provided with Hospital accommodation, Medical attendance, Medicines, Medical comforts and Food free of charge.*

14 *An Emigrant who has a wife still living is not allowed to marry another wife in the Colony unless his marriage with his first wife shall have been legally dissolved; but if he is married to more than one wife in his country he can take them all with him to the Colony and they will then be legally registered and acknowledged as his wives.*

- **a** Give two reasons you know this is not the full contract.
- **b** In which country did labourers sign the contract?
- **c** To which colony does this contract apply?
- **d** What kind of labour are the Indians required to do?
- **e** For how long are employers supposed to provide food for labourers?
- **f** What does the contract say about wives?
- **g** Where are the Indians expected to live?
- **h** How does what the contract says about living arrangements compare to a description from an observer in Fiji of hovels (crude shacks) called coolie lines?
- **i** How many days off work do labourers get?
- **j** Why do you think females and children were also indentured?
- **k** Why would natives of the colony not have signed such contracts?
- **l** Give a short-term effect on the population of the colony of such contracts.
- **m** Give a long-term effect on the population of the colony of such contracts.

# 17 Nation of immigrants

*The USA is referred to as the nation of immigrants, the melting pot (different cultures melt together to form a whole with a common culture) and the salad bowl (while each culture keeps its own distinct qualities like the different ingredients in a salad, the whole has a sense of common identity like the whole salad does).*

*Ellis Island used to be the port of entry for millions of European immigrants; from 1900 to 1914, 5000 to 10,000 came every day.*

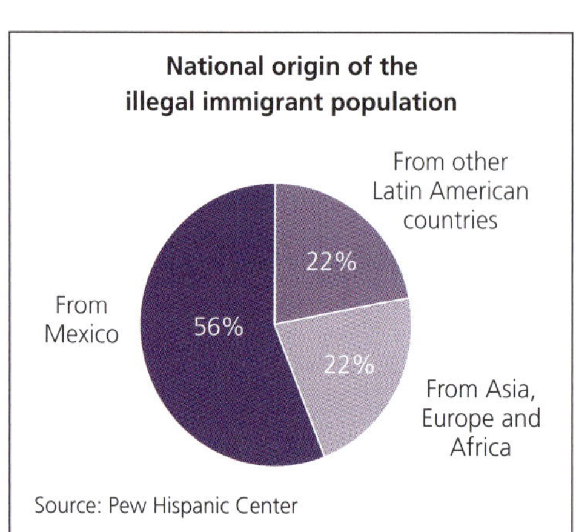


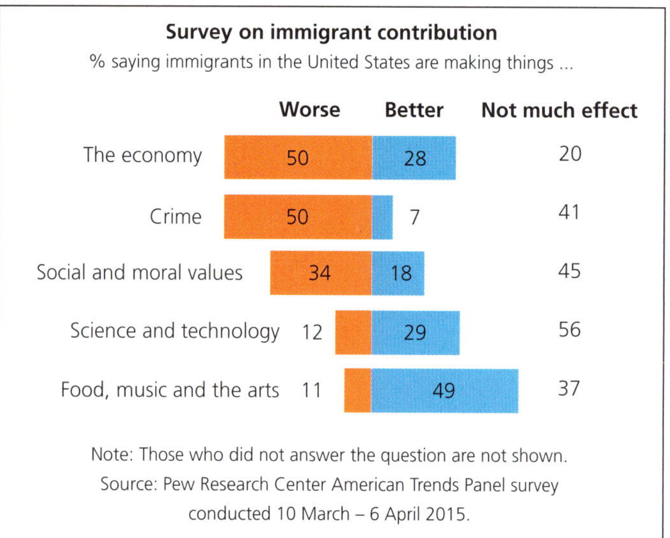


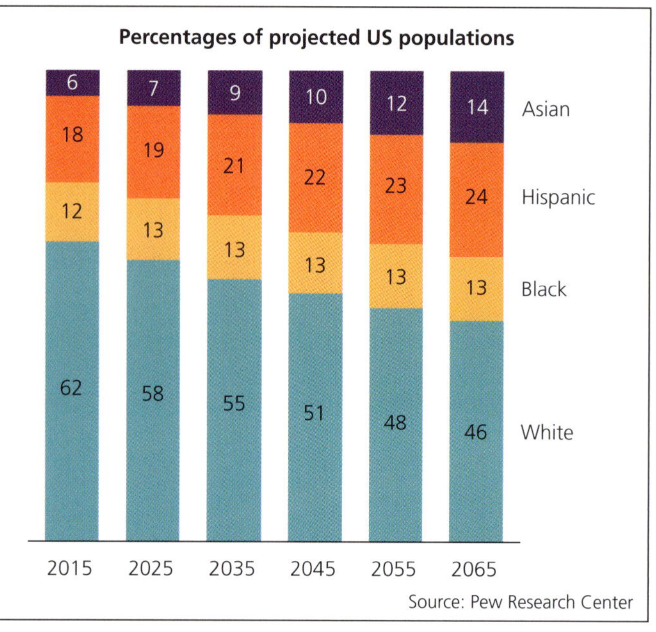






ISBN: 9780170389327

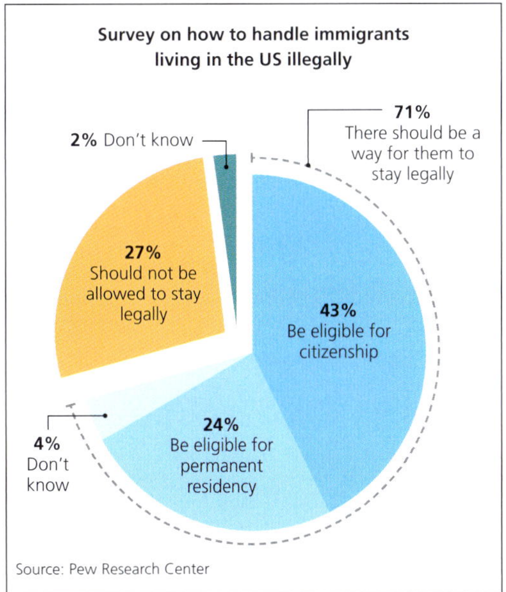


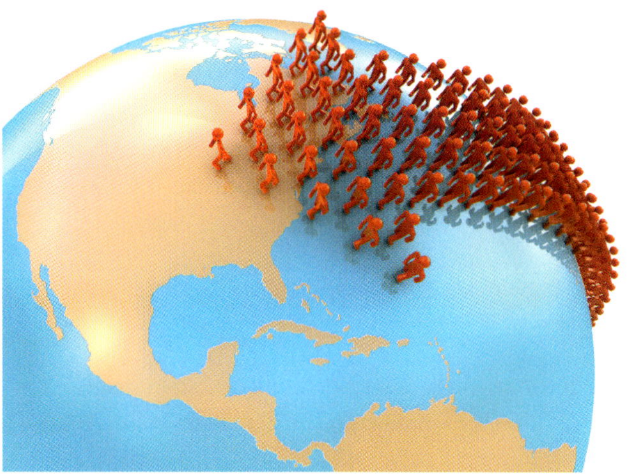

*Each year millions of new immigrants arrive in the USA, legally and illegally, attracted by the democratic system of government, safety from war, and the chance to get a good job and own a house.*

*The USA Immigration Service issues Green Cards to migrants granting them permanent residency. Green cards are not actually green today but the earliest versions of them were.*

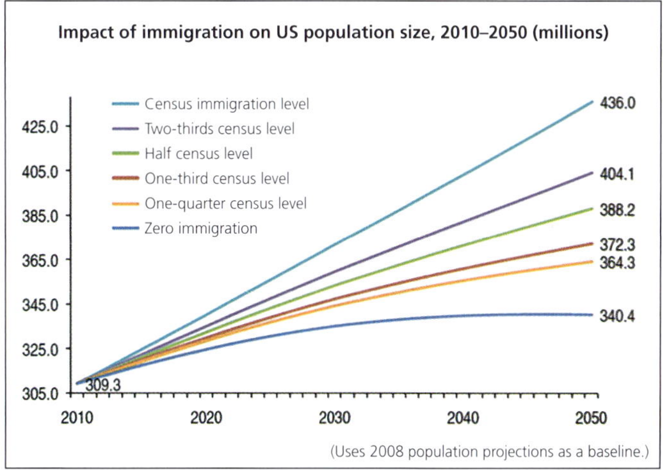


## SKILLS PRACTICE

1 **Survey Percentages** | Study the *Survey on immigrant contribution* and comment on which areas immigrants are considered to be making things better, worse, or not having much effect.

2 **Symbols** | Study the *Percentages of projected US populations* and do the following.

- **a** The colours are symbols for the change in population percentage between 2015 and 2065. Say which symbol refers to which racial or ethnic group.
- **b** Give the name for the groups represented by the following.
  - **i** Originally from place where Spanish is spoken and especially from Latin America, such as Mexico, Guatemala, El Salvador, Honduras.
  - **ii** Having partial or full ancestry from any black racial group of Africa.
  - **iii** Having origins in any of the original peoples of Europe, Middle East or North Africa.
  - **iv** Having ancestral origins in East Asia, South-East Asia or South Asia.

3 **Pie Graph** | Study the pie graph on page 49 and list the things it tells you.

4 **Supplying Data** | Study the graph *Impact of immigration on US population size 2010-2050*. Write out the following sentences and supply the correct data to finish them.

- **a** The title is …
- **b** The data along the *y*-axis shows …
- **c** The data along the *x*-axis shows …
- **d** The word that means a starting point is …
- **e** The word 'projections' means …
- **f** The top line shows that if immigration unfolds as the Census Bureau expects, population will increase from 309.3 in 2010 by the year 2050 to …
- **g** That will be a 41 percent increase in just …
- **h** If immigration is two-thirds of what the Census Bureau expects, the number of additional people in 2050 would be …
- **i** If there is no net immigration, population would still grow by the year 2050 to …
- **j** Even if immigration is half what the Census Bureau expects, the population will still grow by 2050 to …
- **k** If immigration was reduced to only one-third of what the Census Bureau expects, the total population in 2050 would reach …
- **l** That would mean from 2010 an increase of …

5 **Graph Structure** | Study the graph *Survey on how to handle immigrants living in the US illegally*. Explain how the graph is structured and why at first glance it could be confusing.

*From the get-go, the USA has appealed to migrants wanting to better their lives. An old Italian saying is, 'I came to America because the streets were said to be paved with gold. When I arrived, I found out three things. Firstly, I found the streets weren't paved with gold. Secondly, I found the streets weren't paved at all. And thirdly, I found I was expected to pave them.'*



ISBN: 9780170389327

# 18 Westward migration

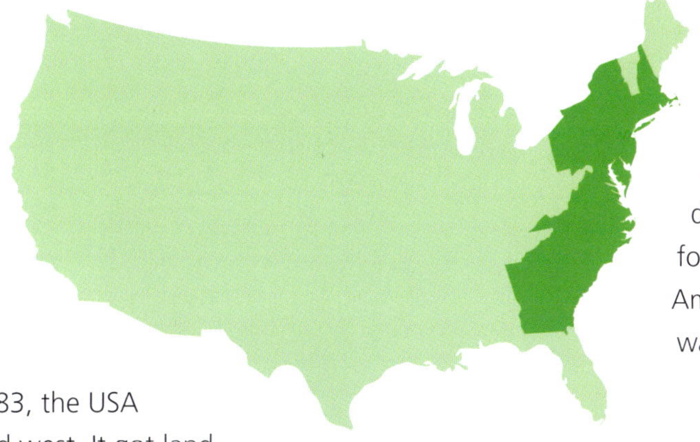

Between 1607 and 1776 Britain established a group of colonies on the eastern side of North America, known as the Thirteen Colonies. In 1776 they declared independence from Britain and formed a nation called the United States of America to fight British troops in them, a war they won in 1783.

After 1783, the USA expanded west. It got land from other European countries such as Spain and France, from neighbouring countries such as Mexico, and from native Indian tribes, by wars and treaties, forced removal of Indian tribes and by buying it. This led to a westward migration of people.

## Push/Pull factors for westward migration

- Belief in Manifest Destiny (see page 54).
- Escape from overcrowded cities in the east.
- Love of nature and wilderness.
- Economic depression in the east.
- Wanting religious freedom.
- Chance to go hunting, trapping, logging.
- Eastern newspaper stories about the wonders of the west.
- New start.
- Runaway slaves got freedom if they went west.
- Escape from diseases.
- Industrialisation in the east meant few jobs for skilled craftsmen.
- Wanting to get rich.
- Belief that industrialisation in the east was making people soft.
- Belief that the west was the land of abundance.
- Popular saying, 'Go west'.
- Missionaries working in Oregon among Indians wrote of region's riches.
- Farmers wanting better land to grow wheat.
- To buy cheap government land and sell it for a profit.
- Wish to explore.
- Land Acts in the west offered free land to those who worked it for a time.
- The discovery of gold in California in 1848.
- Desire for adventure.

*This 1872 painting by John Gast is called* American Progress. *It is about a belief called Manifest Destiny, the idea that the American people had a right from God and a duty to carry their civilisation and liberty all the way across the continent.*

## Results of the migration

The rapid population growth across the US is one of the most important themes in its history; nowhere else has such an immense area been populated so swiftly by individuals and small groups.

It is estimated that by 1855, 300,000 people had arrived in California. The population of San Francisco went from 1000 in 1848 to 298,997 in 1890.

Huge numbers used horse or ox-drawn wagons on trails until rail arrived. An estimated 70,000 migrants set off along trails in just one summer (1852).

Many died from things such as exhaustion, shootings, accidents, drowning, lightning, hailstones, dust, thunderstorms, tornadoes, snowstorms, grassfires, snakebites, diseases, lack of food or water, buffalo herds, head and body lice, mountainous terrain, frostbite, going insane, death of oxen, lack of doctors, self-medication, wolves, bears, mountain lions.

The United States spread from coast to coast.

Less than one percent of the total number of migrants is thought to have died in conflicts with Native Americans, who often helped migrants.

The USA got vast natural resources and ports for trade. It was set on the path towards becoming a superpower.

The so-called Great American Desert, the western Great Plains, was populated.

Native American tribes largely lost lands and their traditional way of life, and ended up in reservations.

 ISBN: 9780170389327

# SKILLS PRACTICE

1 **Categorising** | Sort reasons for the westward migration into push factors and pull factors.

2 **Explaining** | The migrants who went west in wagons like this were known as pioneers. Explain in what way they were pioneers and what sort of dangers they might have had to face.

"With your pioneering spirit, you would be perfect in our marketing department."

3 **Static Image** | Study the 1872 painting and answer the following questions about it.

- **a** When was it painted and what is its title?
- **b** What part of the USA does the right half represent?
- **c** How is this half shown in terms of light and settlement?
- **d** What part of the USA does the left half represent?
- **e** How is this half shown in terms of light and settlement?
- **f** What is the difference between the two halves in terms of geographical features?
- **g** In which direction are people mainly travelling?
- **h** What types of transport are they using?
- **i** The woman in white is Columbia, the goddess of liberty; where has the artist placed her and why?
- **j** In what way is she a symbol of America?
- **k** Why has the artist made it look as if light is coming from her?
- **l** How has the artist suggested she is acting as a guide and defender?
- **m** What technology is she bringing?
- **n** What groups of people are represented?
- **o** What communication systems are shown?
- **p** What are the Indians doing and why are they acting this way?
- **q** What are the bison (buffaloes) doing and why?
- **r** What does it suggest about westward expansion by Americans?

4 **Deducing** | Study the broadside and its caption, and then the following facts about Benjamin Singleton. Say which facts, if any, you could deduce (work out by logical reasoning) from the broadside and caption.

- **a** Benjamin Singleton was black.
- **b** He was born a slave but was no longer one.
- **c** He was known as *old Pap*.
- **d** He escaped to Canada.
- **e** He moved to Michigan where he ran a house that often took in runaway slaves.
- **f** He wanted blacks to own farms.
- **g** He encouraged westward expansion.
- **h** He especially wanted them to go to Kansas.

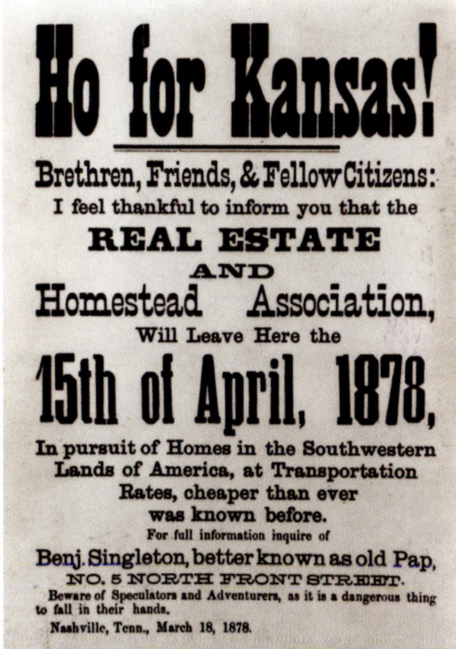

Ho for Kansas!

Brethren, Friends, & Fellow Citizens:
I feel thankful to inform you that the
REAL ESTATE
AND
Homestead Association,
Will Leave Here the
15th of April, 1878,
In pursuit of Homes in the Southwestern Lands of America, at Transportation Rates, cheaper than ever was known before.
For full information inquire of
Benj. Singleton, better known as old Pap,
NO. 5 NORTH FRONT STREET.
Beware of Speculators and Adventurers, as it is a dangerous thing to fall in their hands.
Nashville, Tenn., March 18, 1878.

*A broadside by Benjamin Singleton calling on African Americans to settle in Kansas. 18 March 1878.*

  

i He was involved in a Real Estate and Homestead Association.

j He led a party of migrants in 1878 to Kansas.

k By 1879 he had steered more than 20,000 migrants to Kansas.

5 **Key Ideas** | Read the extract and make a comment about what two key ideas the writer was trying to get across.

> 'The condition of the people of America is so different from aught that we in Europe have an opportunity of observing... They are great travellers, and in general better acquainted with the vast expanse of country ... than the English with their little island. They are also a migrating people, and even when in prosperous circumstances, can contemplate a change of situation, which under our old establishments and fixed habits, none, but the enterprising, would venture upon, when urged by adversity.' (Morris Birkbeck, *Notes on a Journey in America*, 1818)

ISBN: 9780170389327

# 19 Dust Bowl migration

*South Dakota in 1936.*

*Dust storm approaching a settlement in Texas in 1935.*

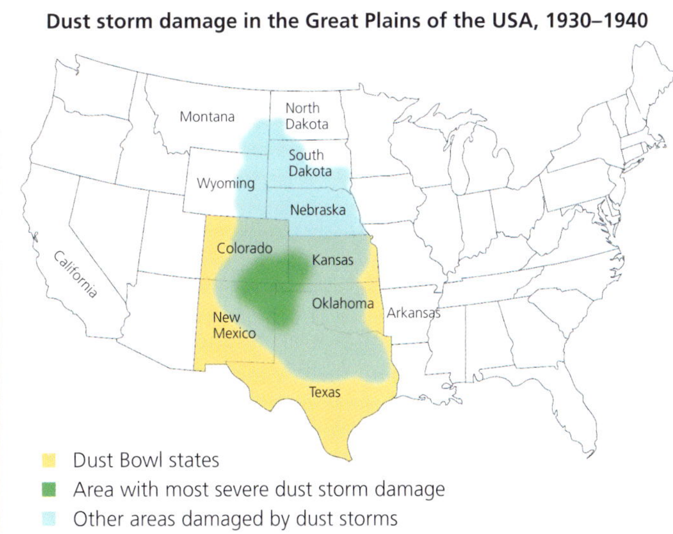


One population migration can lead to another. The westward migration in the USA brought people into the Great Plains and this in turn led to another population migration.

The Great Plains is generally said to be all or part of Colorado, Kansas, Montana, Nebraska, New Mexico, North Dakota, Oklahoma, South Dakota, Texas and Wyoming. Once it was a semi-arid (dry) grassland area of treeless plains. Although it had droughts and high winds, the grasses sustained it by trapping moisture and anchoring soil.

In the 19th century, thousands of migrants arrived. Their cattle, sheep and ploughs destroyed the grasses. Later, farmers had machines such as tractors and combine harvesters, so they decided to convert to crops. This dryland farming relies on moisture in the soil to grow the crops, rather than on rain or irrigation. The farmers did not realise the link between over-farming and land desertification.

Between 1930 and 1940, the southwestern region suffered a drought. Winds blew away the over-farmed soil. Clouds of dust turned the sky dark for days on end. About 400,000 square kilometres of the US heartland became known as the Dust Bowl.

Crops were skittled. The inside and outside of buildings and houses wore dust blankets. Some people died from dust pneumonia, which attacked lungs. Children wore dust masks to and from school. If it was too dangerous to walk home, they had to stay at school overnight. Farm animals died from suffocation. Plagues of spiders, crickets, centipedes, grasshoppers and rabbits arrived.

## Population results

- Between 1930 and 1940, about 3.5 million people migrated from the Dust Bowl area.
- Many migrants moved to California because it had a bigger population and better job opportunities.
- This migration was during an economic depression when internal migration rates for other parts of the country were low and when high unemployment made migration risky.
- Whites made up roughly 95 percent of migrants. Gender was fairly evenly balanced. Some African Americans migrated, but usually for cities in the north.
- Hobos were migrants who had no vehicles and no money for train or bus tickets. Many were killed or injured as they tried to jump on to trains, and some were killed by guards hired by railways to keep them away.
- Other states sometimes tried to stop migrants, especially poor ones, coming to live there. Locals sometimes beat up migrants camped on roadsides and burned their shelters down. California had an Act that made it a crime to bring in poor people. The Los Angeles police chief sent police to act as bouncers at the state border. The press called them 'the Bum Brigade'. In 1941 the US Supreme Court ruled that states had no right to stop the migration of poor people into their states.

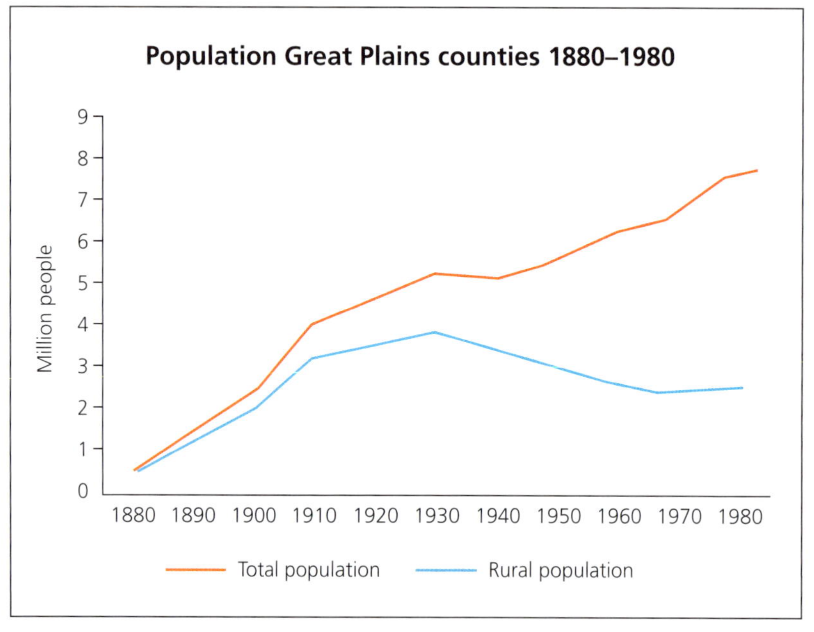


- When migrants reached California and found most farmland was in large corporate farms which offered poor pay and poor living conditions, and where crops were not the familiar wheat but fruit, nuts and vegetables, many gave up farming. They set up near cities in shacktowns called Little Oklahomas or Okievilles. They built houses from what they could scavenge, living with polluted water and no plumbing or electricity. Even after they built proper houses and became part of the community, they faced discrimination in the job market and were still called Okies and Arkies no matter where they came from.
- 'Very erect and primly severe, [a man] addressed the slumped driver of a rolling wreck that screamed from every hinge, bearing and coupling. *"California's relief rolls are overcrowded now. No use to come farther,"* he cried. The half-collapsed driver ignored him — merely turned his head to be sure his numerous family was still with him. They were so tightly wedged in, that escape was impossible. *"There really is nothing for you here,"* the neat trooperish young man went on. *"Nothing, really nothing."* And the forlorn man on the moaning car looked at him, dull, emotionless, incredibly weary, and said: *"So? Well, you ought to see what they got where I come from."* ' (1935 extract from *Collier's* magazine)



ISBN: 9780170389327

# SKILLS PRACTICE

1 **Graph or Table Making** | Create a graph or table to show the number of dust storms.

Dust storms in the region between 1932 and 1940 rose to 72 in 1937. 1936 had 68 and 1938 had 61. The lowest number was 14 in 1932 followed by 17 in 1940. 1934 had 22, 1933 had 38, 1939 had 30 and 1935 had 10 more than that.

2 **Definitions** | Prepare a definition for each of the following.

- **a** dryland farming
- **b** the Great Plains
- **c** drought
- **d** dust pneumonia
- **e** shacktown
- **f** Dust Bowl
- **g** Okie
- **h** Bum Brigade
- **i** Okieville

3 **Reasoning** | Make reasoned sentences about the Dust Bowl migration by explaining each of the following.

- **a** Human actions caused the Dust Bowl.
- **b** It was an internal migration.
- **c** It was an interregional migration.
- **d** It was voluntary.
- **e** Many migrants went to California.
- **f** Many migrants gave up farming when they got to California.
- **g** Migrants were called Okies and Arkies.
- **h** Some people thought dust storms had brought the end of the world.
- **i** In 1941 the US Supreme Court probably stopped future conflict.
- **j** The death rate of hobos was high.

4 **Contributions** | Explain what information each of the following contribute to your understanding of the Dust Bowl Migration.

- **a** The dust storm damage map.
- **b** The population graph.
- **c** The 1935 *Collier's* extract.
- **d** The images.

5 **Explaining the How** | In either a diagram or writing, explain how people's management of resources can impact on population.

# 20 Impact of migration on places

## The causes

1 New Orleans was a city and major port in the USA state of Louisiana on the east and west banks of Mississippi River about 169 km upriver from the Gulf of Mexico. Built on soft sand, silt and clay, it was mostly below sea-level and surrounded by water. Defence walls called levees protected it.

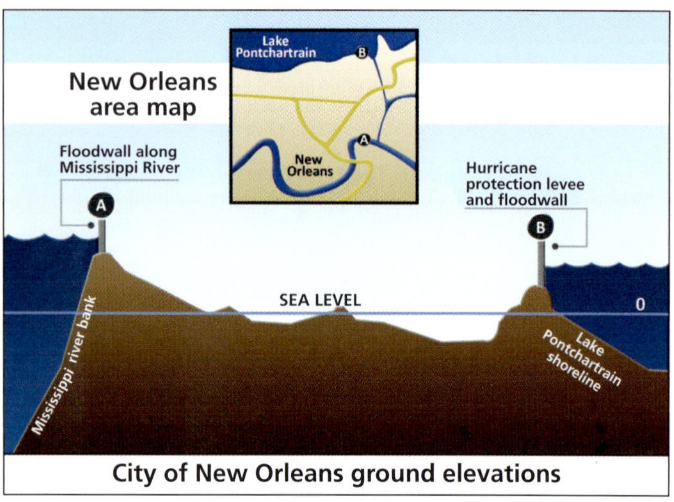

2 A hurricane is a cyclone, typhoon or tropical storm with heavy rains and strong winds that rotate in a circle. New Orleans is affected by the Atlantic hurricane season, which runs from June through November each year. During a hurricane, a storm surge can build up in Lake Pontchartrain and water can spill into New Orleans.

3 In August 2005 one of the worst hurricanes ever, called Katrina, tracked over the Gulf of Mexico. It ended up killing 1836 people. When it went through New Orleans, the levees could not cope with all the extra water and many collapsed. About 80 percent of the city was flooded to depths of up to six metres. This was the worst civil engineering disaster in USA history.

## The event

1 As Katrina approached, about a million people in Louisiana had been evacuated from its path.

2 Up to 100,000 people in New Orleans had no access to transport and had to stay put.

ISBN: 9780170389327

## The results

1. There is still no final data on exactly what happened to the population because neither the local nor federal governments had systems to properly track it.
2. What is known is that the migration of people because of Katrina changed places that people migrated from, such as New Orleans, and also changed places that people migrated to, such as Houston, Texas.

## The impact on New Orleans

## The impact on Houston

- The city of Houston got more Katrina migrants than anywhere else in the USA.
- About 250,000 arrived. A year later an estimated 150,000 were still there. Probably about 100,000 are there permanently.
- A survey of 2006 showed that about a quarter of the migrants lived in high-crime and high-poverty neighbourhoods.
- The region struggled to cope. Housing was scarce and many migrants could not afford it. Migrants overwhelmed schools, transport systems and medical programmes.
- There was much kindness from strangers, such as paying for migrants' meals at cafes and diners. Thousands of residents of Houston volunteered to help in a multi-million dollar campaign to house, feed and give health care to migrants.
- Some Houston residents were cautious of Katrina migrants, who were largely poor and black. They complained of a crime wave. Statistics later proved that was not true, although it took years to get accurate data.

- Some residents said the 'Katrina illegal immigrants' should be sent home.
- Migrants stayed linked by their culture and set up music bands and churches. They called Houston 'New Orleans West'.
- Migrants brought their traumatic experience with them. Houses had flooded so quickly that many residents were trapped in water up to their necks, some for days, waiting for rescue. Many migrants said their health had gone downhill and this made it hard to look for jobs. This put financial stress on medical systems.
- The percentage of Houstonians saying the migrant arrival was a good thing for the city was 32 percent in 2006 and 7 percent in 2008. The percentage saying it was a bad thing for Houston was 70 percent in 2008 and 58 percent in 2010.

## SKILLS PRACTICE

1 **Explaining Population Movements |** Study the graph and explain the two population movements it shows.

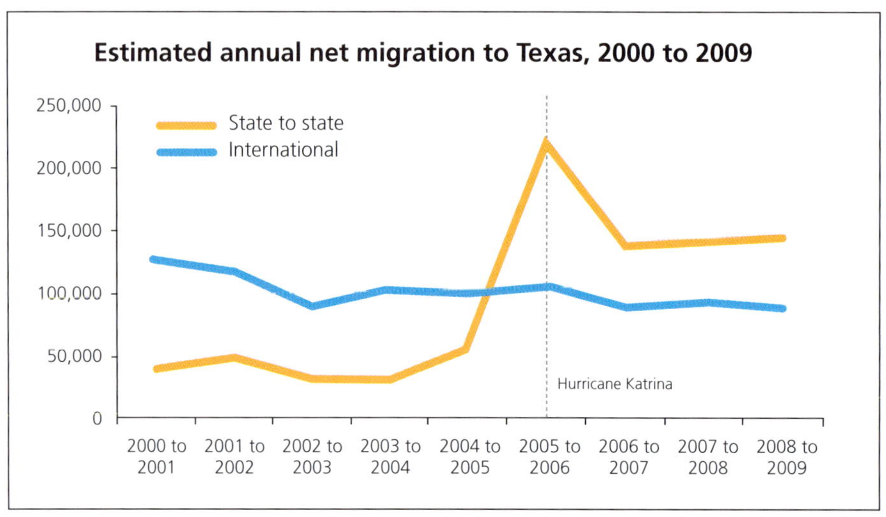


2 **Impact Map |** Look at the Nasa image of New Orleans (on page 63) a week after Katrina and answer the following questions about it.

**a** What is the source of the image?
**b** What kind of image is it?
**c** In what month was the image made?
**d** What is the name of the river and where is it located?
**e** What is the name of the lake and where is it located?
**f** What colour are the flooded areas?
**g** Why would not owning a car have been a disadvantage after Katrina?
**h** What evidence is there that the water of the lake remains clouded with silt stirred up when Hurricane Katrina passed overhead on 29 August?
**i** By this time the breaches in the levees that let water flow in to New Orleans have been sealed; has this fixed the situation?
**j** Where is there some dry land?
**k** In much of the city, what are the only things visible above the water?
**l** What does the photo suggest is the cause of so many migrants leaving New Orleans?



ISBN: 9780170389327

New Orleans, a week after Hurricane Katrina. (NASA)

ISBN: 9780170389327  

**3 Population Graph |** Study the population graph and answer the questions about it.

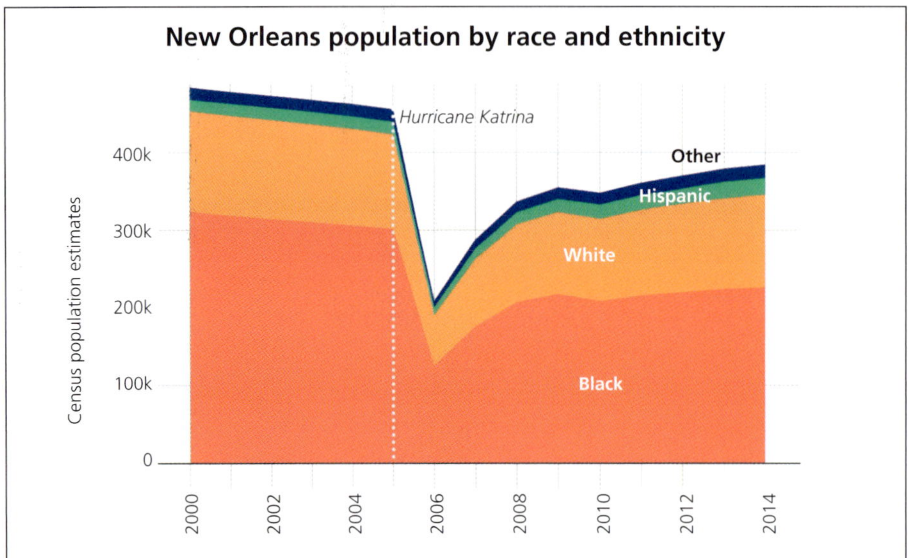


- **a** What is the source of the graph?
- **b** What is the title of the graph?
- **c** On which axis is the letter k and what does it stand for?
- **d** Which specific sentence in the text does the graph provide evidence for?
- **e** Give two other pieces of information the graph shows about the impact of Katrina on New Orleans.
- **f** Does the graph suggest the following data is most likely to be true or most likely to be untrue?

> In New Orleans, the Census Bureau estimated that in 2012 African Americans still represented the majority of the city's population at 59 percent, down from 67 in 2000, while there were 14,984 fewer whites and 4830 more Hispanics.

**4 Oral Presentation |** Make a short oral presentation about the New Orleans ground elevations cross-section diagram. Never assume your audience is familiar with anything; always explain even the most basic points.

**5 Assessing Impact |** In any format, such as writings or labelled diagrams, show the impact of Katrina migration on New Orleans (a place they left from) and Houston (a place they went to).



ISBN: 9780170389327

# 21 Migrants punch above their weight

By 2016 there were 3.4 million Indians in the USA. Whether they stayed there, or migrated back to India, many had done so well and become so respected in their host and home countries they were said to be punching above their weight.

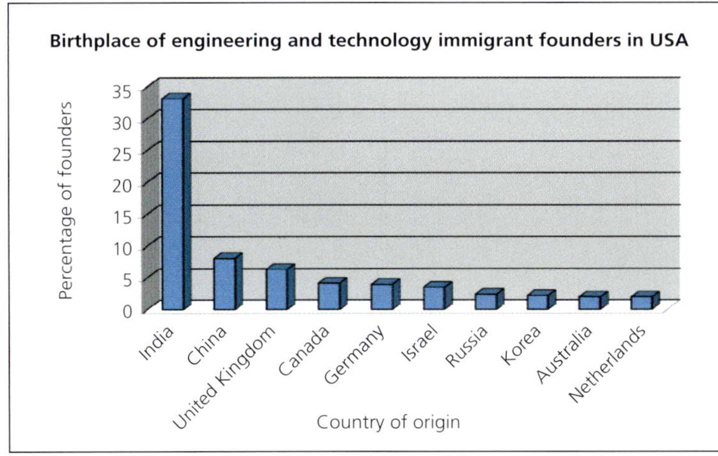

A recent study showed that Indians were the greatest number of the immigrant tech-company founders in the USA, having founded more startups than the next four groups.

In 2016, Y Combinator (YC), which is seen as a breeding ground for emerging tech giants, for the first time took up three domestic startups into its summer batch. They were all Indian — Innov8, a co-working space; JustRide, a self-drive car rental app; and Meesho, an app for sellers on Facebook and WhatsApp. YC invests $120,000 in startups for a 7 percent equity stake across two batches every year, and is a top place for venture capitalists who pick companies to fund.

Thousands of Indians had migrated to Silicon Valley, which is a nickname for the southern part of the San Francisco Bay area in California. 'Valley' refers to the Santa Clara Valley where the region is centred, and 'Silicon' refers to the fact that this is where the silicon-based integrated circuit, the microprocessor, and the microcomputer, and other key technologies, were developed. It houses many of the world's largest high-tech corporations and thousands of startup companies. It accounts for about one-third of all the venture capital investment in the USA.

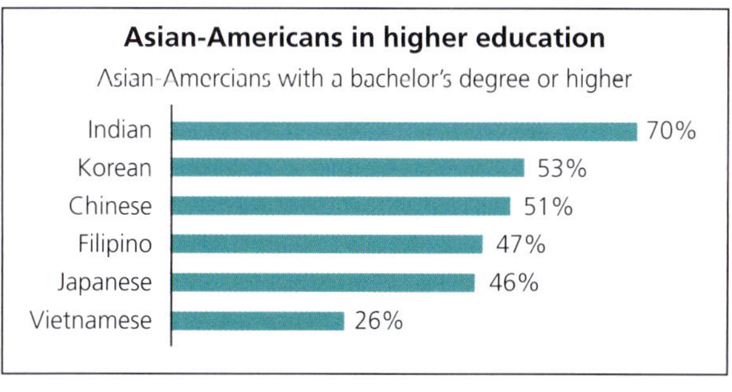


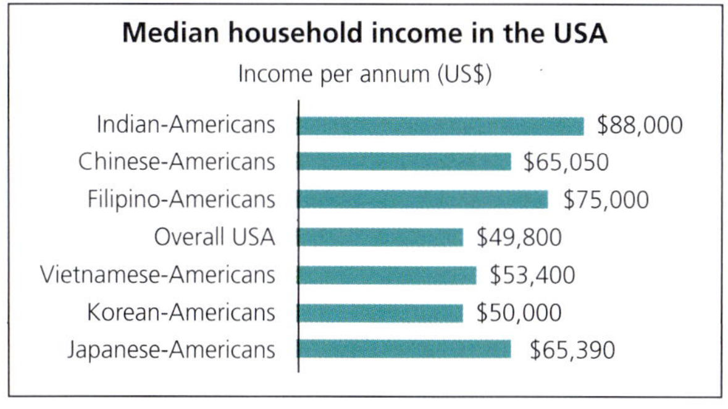


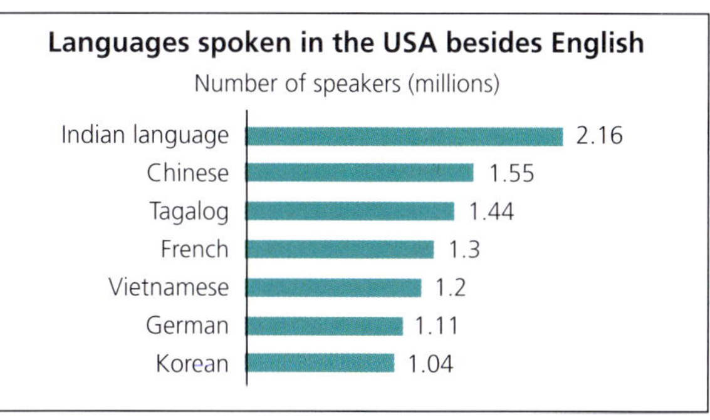

Indian migration to the USA began in the 1960s when the USA was reacting to the Soviet Union taking the lead in the space race. The USA decided it needed to import scientists and engineers to catch up. It therefore removed national origin as the basis of immigration and replaced it with technical skills and expertise. This was good for India because it had many trained people who could not get jobs in their fields in India. In the 1970s and 80s, waves of graduates from India's top engineering colleges migrated to the USA.

By 2016 there was some reverse migration with Indians leaving the USA to return to India.

## Push-Pull factors for Indian migration to the USA

- Highly trained IT Indians needed jobs.
- India's population had reached one billion by 1999.
- Limited opportunities in India.
- Desire to work hard for success to help the family.
- Indians learn English at school and so cope well in global business.
- Previous migrants built a strong support network for other Indian migrants, with successful Indians and angel funders (investors in small startups or entrepreneurs) willing to mentor newcomers.
- Desire and ability to enrol in USA higher education.
- Higher-paid jobs means money can be sent home to help family.
- Higher standard of living.
- Give children overseas experience.
- Indian culture accepted, such as celebration of Diwali Festival of Lights.

## Push-Pull factors for reverse Indian migration to India from the USA

- Desire to help solve some of the big problems facing India.
- The number of startups in India is expected to be over 11,500 by 2020.
- Lower cost of living in India.
- Need to take care of parents.
- Better family life available in India.
- Fear that family name might die out in India.
- Senior executives have enough money to go home to launch startups.
- Venture capital funds now available in India for startups.
- Many migrants were from lower castes and have gained respect by being so successful overseas.
- Returning migrants can persuade their colleagues to go back to India too.
- Pride that India is home to millions of IT workers and the numbers of Indians connected to the internet is growing rapidly.



ISBN: 9780170389327

# SKILLS PRACTICE

1 **Jargon** | Create a way to show that you understand the jargon (specialist words) below and how they fit into the story of Indian migration to and from the USA. An easy way is to use them in sentences.

| | | | |
|---|---|---|---|
| angel funder | startup | key technologies | YC |
| Silicon Valley | Diwali | venture capital | IT |
| entrepreneurs | capitalists | reverse migration | tech giant |

2 **Arguing a Case** | Prepare some notes on whether or not you think the following statement is accurate.

> Sputnik launched India immigration to the United States.

3 **Making a Graph** | Arrange the following data from a recent USA study into a graph.

> 76 percent of Indian immigrants (ages 25 and over) had a bachelor's degree or higher, compared with 28 percent of all immigrants over 25 and 30 percent of native-born adults.

4 **Defending a Decision** | As an Indian migrant to Silicon Valley, you have decided to migrate back to India. You have received an email from a colleague at Microsoft wondering if you are a deserter. Write an email that you could send back defending your decision.

5 **Neutral Versus Emotional** | Explain which of the following statements are neutral and which are emotional.

- **a** Top talent migrants from India are returning home to India's e-commerce giants like Flipkart and Snapdeal.
- **b** Instead of getting frustrated by lack of facilities in India and migrating to the USA, Indians should show more loyalty and guts and help make things better in India.
- **c** The Indian-American population rose 76 percent in the early years of the 21st century.
- **d** A recent study showed only 9 percent of adult Indian Americans lived in poverty, compared with 12 percent of Asian Americans overall and 13 percent of the US population.
- **e** India's smartphone penetration rate in the past was ridiculously hopeless at 30 percent, much lower than China's amazing 95 percent.
- **f** Indian immigrants tend to have much higher educational attainment compared to both foreign- and native-born populations.

# 22 Irish diaspora

*The island of Ireland is located to the west of England, Scotland and Wales. One of the issues that impacted on it in the past, is impacting on it in the present, and will impact on it in the future, is called the Irish diaspora.*

Diaspora means a group migration from a homeland that has scattered into different countries.

The Government of Ireland (which today excludes Northern Ireland, which is part of Britain) says Irish diaspora means Irish who live outside Ireland, while other groups say it means everybody who claims some Irish ancestry. This is why the Irish diaspora estimated numbers range from three million to 70 or 100 million.

No other country in Europe has been as affected by diaspora over the last two centuries as Ireland.

'Most countries send out oil or iron, steel or gold, or some other crop, but Ireland has had only one export and that is its people.' (John F. Kennedy on his US presidential visit to Ireland, June 1963)

In 2014, the Irish Government appointed a Minister of State for the Diaspora as an official acknowledgement that all Irish people outside Ireland are important and not forgotten.

## Everybody's Irish on St Patrick's Day

It has been estimated that up to one in four people in Britain have some Irish ancestry.

By 1890, 40 percent of Irish-born people had migrated to other countries.

In their 2011 census, over 2 million people in Australia said they were of Irish descent, which was over 10 percent of Australia's population.

By 1851, about a quarter of the population of England's Liverpool were born in Ireland and more than half the people of Canada's Toronto were Irish.

Irish communities are found all over the world, such as 7000 first-generation Irish in the United Arab Emirates, and more than 500,000 people of Irish descent in Argentina.

By 2000, an estimated 80 million people worldwide claimed some Irish descent and more than 36 million Americans claimed Irish as their main ethnicity.

By 2016, an estimated 100 plus million people worldwide claimed some Irish descent.

The Irish diaspora spread Irish culture around the world. During the 17th century many Irish went to work in the Caribbean and there today are Irish place names such as Cork Hill, and Irish surnames such as Riley, while some islands have a national holiday on St Patrick's Day.



ISBN: 9780170389327

# The Irish in New Zealand

Before 1921 Ireland was one country. From 1921 it had Northern Ireland and the Republic of Ireland (independent country).

| New Zealand census year | Number born in Ireland |
|---|---|
| 1858 | 4554 |
| 1901 | 43,524 |
| **Northern Ireland** | |
| 1951 | 8817 |
| 1976 | 9694 |
| 2001 | 4095 |
| 2006 | 4776 |
| 2013 | 4710 |
| **Republic of Ireland** | |
| 1951 | 6423 |
| 1976 | 5622 |
| 2001 | 6726 |
| 2006 | 6888 |
| 2013 | 9042 |
| **Ireland (undefined)** | |
| 1951 | 1932 |
| 1976 | 1877 |

*The Irish potato famine of 1845–52 caused over a million people to migrate from Ireland. Over 95 percent of them crossed the Atlantic to the USA.*

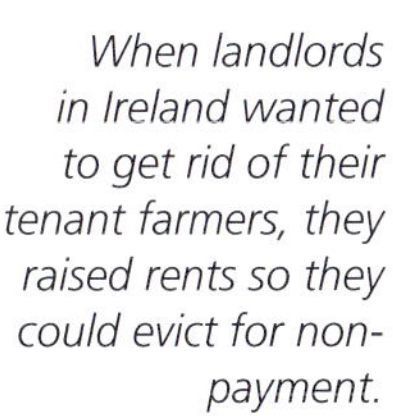

*When landlords in Ireland wanted to get rid of their tenant farmers, they raised rents so they could evict for non-payment.*

## SKILLS PRACTICE

**1 Assessing Suitability** | You are gathering sources on the Irish diaspora and have found an image which you think could illustrate the Bridge of Tears. Read the following information and then assess the suitability of the image.

In Ireland there is a small stone bridge, called Bridge of Tears, over a stream. In the 19th and early 20th centuries families walked to the bridge with their loved ones who were leaving and had to cross the bridge on their way to the port of Derry, which was the main departure point for migrants from Donegal. For many, the bridge was the last place they would see their family and friends.

**2 References** | State what the following refer to in the text.

**a** 43,524 **b** 36 million **c** 40 **d** 70 million
**e** 1963 **f** 500,000 **g** 95 **h** 17th
**i** 1945 **j** 8817 **k** 9042 **l** 2014

3 **Most Likely** | Study the image and give the 'most likely' for each of the following features about it.

- **a** The country.
- **b** The main push factor for migrants.
- **c** The main food source for the villagers.
- **d** The approximate date.
- **e** The port they are going to if leaving from Donegal.
- **f** Overseas destination of migrants.

*A priest blesses migrants leaving during the big famine.*

4 **Plus-Minus Chart** | Find the answers to the following questions on the chart.

- **a** These figures are for the Republic of Ireland. Why is 'Irish' in the title confusing?
- **b** What is the difference between immigration and emigration?
- **c** Why does one set of figures have a minus sign in front of them?
- **d** Which years had more immigrants than emigrants?
- **e** Which years had more emigrants than immigrants?
- **f** What happened to emigration figures during the Great Recession, a time of financial crisis that officially went from December 2007 to June 2009?
- **g** Of the people who emigrated in 2015, 43.6 percent were Irish nationals. Is that figure likely to have been 35,300 or 53,300?
- **h** Would this chart be useful to show the Irish diaspora at this time? Give reasons for your answer.

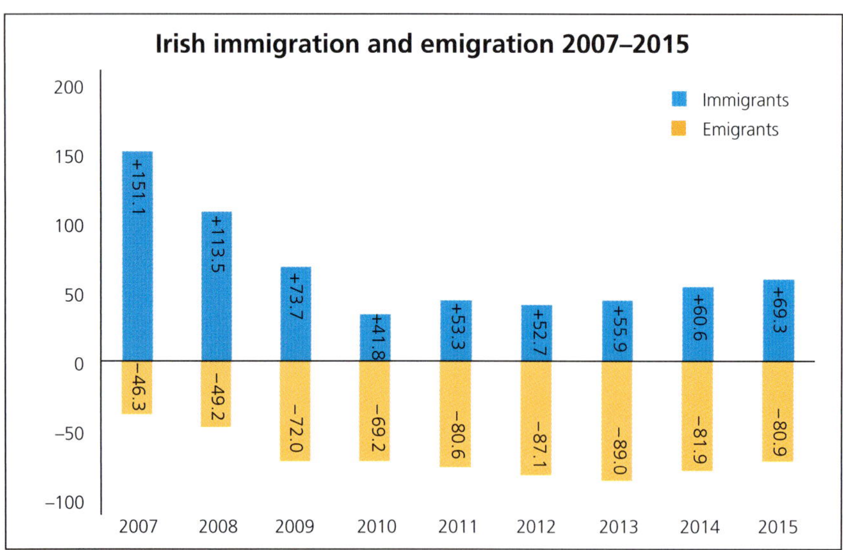


5 **Combining Elements** | Explain how you would combine three elements — an outline map of Ireland, a symbol of Irish people, and a symbol for the world — into a drawing to show the meaning of the Irish diaspora.



ISBN: 9780170389327

# 23 Early Polynesian migration to Aotearoa

1 Polynesia means many islands. The term is used for a region of the Pacific that is shaped roughly like a triangle. Indigenous (native, first) people who live in the region are called Polynesians.

2 Polynesians sailed canoes and used weather systems, ocean currents, winds and stars to navigate. New Zealand was the last big land mass they reached.

Hawaii
POLYNESIA
Tuvalu
Tokelau
Samoa
Marquesas Is.
Cook Is.
Tuamotu Arch.
Society Is.
Mangareva
Tonga
Austral Is.
Kermadec Is.
Easter Island
New Zealand

3 Nobody knows the exact date for the Polynesian arrival in New Zealand but historians think it was most likely the 13th century.

4 These migrants were the ancestors of today's Maori. They found no people in Aotearoa which is why Maori are called indigenous.

5 Maori oral tradition told of their ancestral home being Hawaiki but nobody knows exactly where that was. Historians say that evidence such as DNA, radiocarbon dating, language, tradition, canoe reconstructions, computer voyaging and artefacts (man-made objects) show migrants most likely came from East Polynesia.

6 They possibly did not come from just one particular place. They may have come over several generations or centuries. They possibly included 70–100 women. When they stopped making return voyages to East Polynesia, the migrants in Aotearoa were cut off from the rest of the world.

## Possible push and pull factors

- Wanting to escape war in their homeland.
- Younger family members wanting more responsibility.
- Needing more space (but there is no evidence of overcrowding being a factor).
- Drift voyages, meaning they arrived by accident (but the most popular belief today is they arrived on purpose and brought settlers, plants and animals).
- Being banished from their homeland.
- Wanting to go exploring and have adventures.
- Needing more resources such as food (but the migrants were good food growers so did not depend totally on hunting and gathering food resources that they could have used up in their homeland).
- Wanting to be heroes who found new lands.
- Wanting to know what was to the south of their homeland.
- Knowing that land lay south of them because they saw migrating birds such as the long-tailed cuckoo that comes to New Zealand to breed.

## Older ideas

Until the 1960s, students learned a different version about the earliest migrants. It said that in AD 750 the Polynesian explorer Kupe discovered Aotearoa. No humans lived there. In AD 1000–1100, the Polynesian explorers Toi and Whatonga visited and found a people called Moriori living in it. In AD 1350 a great fleet of seven canoes left from the Tahitian region and brought migrants to Aotearoa. The migrants took New Zealand from the Moriori.

Modern research suggests that the Moriori were actually a group of Maori who migrated from New Zealand to the Chatham Islands, and developed their own culture.

## SKILLS PRACTICE

1 **Relative Distances** | Draw a map to show approximate locations of the following to each other: New Zealand, Chathams, Kermadecs, Tonga, Samoa, Society Islands, Hawaii, Cook Islands.

2 **Understanding Actions** | Explain, such as by writing sentences or drawing diagrams, what the following actions mean.

- **a** navigating a canoe
- **b** radiocarbon dating
- **c** using DNA
- **d** banishing someone
- **e** using up resources
- **f** drift voyaging
- **g** developing a culture
- **h** hunting and gathering
- **i** being indigenous

3 **Looking at a Caricature** | Study the caricature and answer the questions about it.

- **a** Who drew it and when?
- **b** Why would the title be considered wrong today?
- **c** Which features are exaggerated?
- **d** What animal has come with the migrants?
- **e** What creatures have come to meet the migrants?
- **f** How are the creatures behaving?
- **g** What is the reaction of the arrivals to the creatures?
- **h** What has been a food source for the migrants?
- **i** How accurate do you think it is?

*This early 20th century drawing by Trevor Lloyd is described as a caricature — an exaggeration of features for comic effect. The title is* The Arrival of the Maories.

4 **Making Notes** | Make about half a page to one page of notes about the main points in this unit.

5 **Understanding Revisionism** | Revisionism is when historians re-interpret the historical record to take into account new evidence that comes to light. Give two examples of revisionism from this unit and say how the revisionism has changed the historical record in both examples.



ISBN: 9780170389327

# 24 White immigration policy

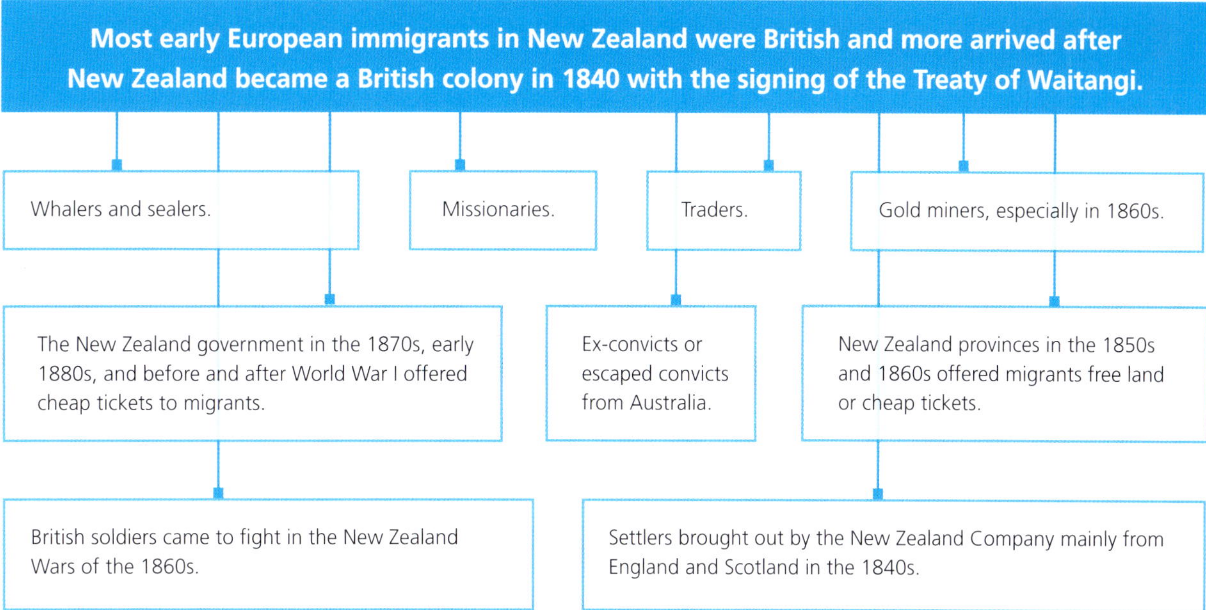


The early British settlers believed they should make New Zealand a 'Britain of the South'. Many believed that the culture of white people was superior and so they should make it harder for those they called 'race aliens', such as Chinese and Indians, to get into the country. Such an idea is known as a white immigration policy.

This policy of trying to make New Zealand British and white lasted until about the early 1970s.

Not everyone in New Zealand agreed with this policy.

Some other countries, such as Australia and Canada, also had this policy.

## Examples

**1881** Number of Chinese who could arrive on one ship was one for every 10 tons of the ship's weight. Chinese had to pay a poll tax to enter. (A poll is a head; a poll tax was a tax on a person.)

**1888** Ratio of immigrants to ship tonnage was one Chinese per 100 tons.

**1896** Ratio was one Chinese per 200 tons. Poll tax was increased.

**1899** Banned entry of immigrants who were not of British or Irish parentage and who could not fill out an application form 'in any European language' — which in practice meant English.

**1907** Chinese had to pass an additional English-language reading test by reading 100 words of English in front of customs officials.

ISBN: 9780170389327

**1931** Aliens from Europe banned from entering New Zealand. Exceptions were if they had guaranteed jobs, or a lot of money, or knowledge and skills 'which would enable them to rehabilitate readily, but without detriment to any resident of New Zealand'.

**1946** Preference was for immigrants to be of British stock. If numbers of British immigrants fell short, people from Scandinavia or northern Europe would be considered.

**1947** Free passage granted to suitable British people from armed forces, and assisted passage to suitable young, single migrants.

**1950** This scheme was extended to include Dutch, Danish, Swiss, Austrian and German people under 35 years.

**1974 on** Officially, but not always officially, applicants granted permanent entry on basis of demand for their skills and qualifications.

## SKILLS PRACTICE

1 **Identify** | Find as many push and pull factors as you can for immigrants coming to New Zealand.

2 **Primary Sources** | Study the table and graph and answer the questions about them.

**Busby's estimates of the European population of New Zealand, February 1836**

| District | Males | Females | Children |
|---|---|---|---|
| North Cape to Whangaroa | 7 | 4 | 3 |
| Whangaroa | 15 | 2 | 5 |
| Bay of Islands | 102 | 40 | 61 |
| Hokianga | 84 | 16 | 73 |
| 'All places south of Bay of Islands and Hokianga' | 73 | 11 | 16 |
| South Island | 180 | – | – |
| Chatham and Stewart Islands | 30 | – | – |
| **Totals** | **491** | **73** | **158** |

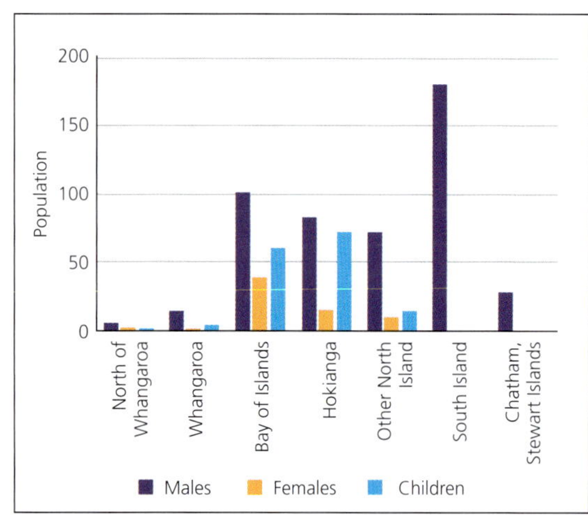


*James Busby was an official called the British Resident, in the Bay of Islands. Because he prepared the table and graph himself while he was living there, they are called primary sources.*

a Why is Busby's table a primary source?

b Why did he say it was an estimate?

c How many adult males were there?

d How many adult females were there?

e What was the approximate ratio of adult men to adult women?

f What is the total population?

g Most of those in the South Island lived in the Marlborough Sounds; what does that suggest about their occupation?

h 'Three-quarters of those in the North Island lived in the Bay of Islands, Hokianga, or further north.' Is that a true statement or a false one?

i Why would James Busby have been the one to make a census of population?

j Do you find it easier to get an idea of the European population in New Zealand in 1836 from the graph or from the table? Give a reason for your answer.



ISBN: 9780170389327

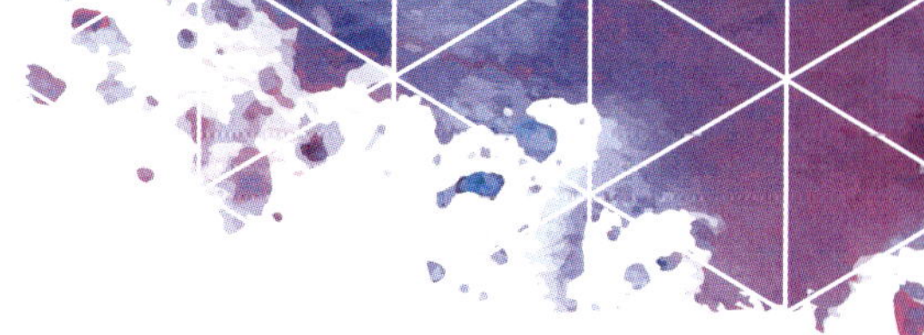

**3 Official Document** | Read the extract and answer the questions about it.

> 'Our immigration is based firmly on the principle that we are and intend to remain a country of European development. It is inevitably discriminatory against Asians — indeed against all persons who are not wholly of European race and colour. Whereas we have done much to encourage immigration from Europe, we do everything to discourage it from Asia.' (1953 Department of External Affairs memorandum)

- **a** What word means a basic idea or rule?
- **b** What word means 'can't be avoided'?
- **c** What word means 'making unfair distinctions between people'?
- **d** What word means the opposite of encourage?
- **e** What is the source of this extract?
- **f** What reason is given for the principle?
- **g** Provide four examples from past practice as evidence of the principle.

**4 Historical Cartoon** | Study the cartoon and answer the questions about it.

- **a** Who are the four people?
- **b** What is the weapon?
- **c** When was the weapon made and how did it work?
- **d** What role is Public Opinion playing?
- **e** Which two are most likely to be immigrants?
- **f** What is the reaction of the immigrants?
- **g** How has the cartoonist shown this reaction?
- **h** Would you expect to see such a cartoon published today? Give a reason for your answer.

**5 Historical Photo** | Study the photo and say if you can find any evidence for the statements below, and if so, what the evidence is.

- **a** Even though public meetings called for a ban on Chinese migrants, Chinese miners came to the Otago fields.
- **b** Very few Chinese women migrated with Chinese male gold miners.
- **c** Not all non-Chinese people in New Zealand were anti-Chinese.
- **d** Miners built houses from available material on the land.
- **e** Chinese were excluded from the Old Age Pensions Act of 1898.
- **f** Chinese miners were able to save money.
- **g** The Chinese were said to give the opium pipe to little boys to smoke.
- **h** The Chinese were, said a politician, 'dirty, miserly, ignorant, a shirker of social duty, and a danger to public health'.
- **i** In 1857, before a Chinese person had arrived in the area, Nelson set up an anti-Chinese committee.

*Chinese gold miners with a church reverend outside a sod house at Tuapeka in Otago about 1900.*

# 25 Hot migration issue

## Essential ideas about migration to and from New Zealand

1. New Zealand's population has always been helped by immigration.
2. Every month, Government releases new figures on migration, which means the issue has high visibility.
3. New Zealand usually gains more people from long-term arrivals than it loses from long-term departures.
4. Net migration is calculated from permanent and long-term arrivals less permanent and long-term departures.
5. Immigration is changing the face of New Zealand and causing debate.
6. It is very hard for immigrants to get permanent residency in New Zealand.
7. An increase in immigration can put pressure on infrastructure, such as housing, schools, hospitals and roads.
8. Auckland, Wellington and Christchurch have been the greatest receivers of migrants.
9. New Zealand has a low population density. This is a reason many say it could take a lot more immigrants than it does.
10. New Zealand is a world leader in ensuring its economic immigrants are employed. Its system for immigration is held in high regard by international organisations and some other countries have copied it.

## How statistics need background understanding

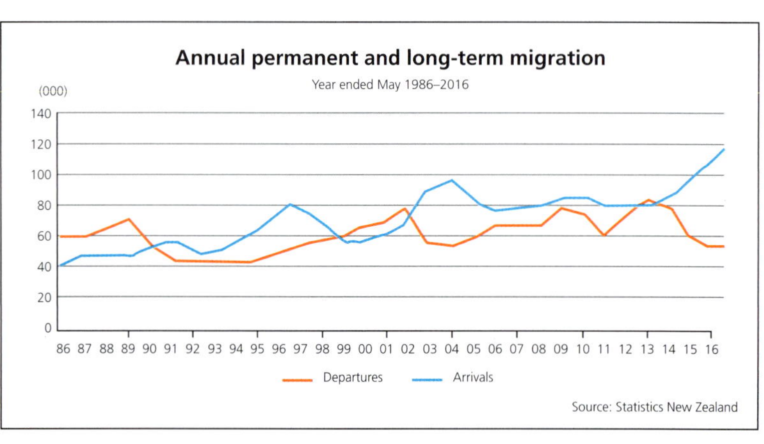


Here are some background comments from experts on migration that may have a bearing on how people view such graphs.

1. The figures include everybody who is staying or leaving for more than 12 months. That can give wrong impressions such as overseas students coming to study but intending to leave after finishing their study.
2. More than half the people who immigrate leave within 13 years.
3. Some Kiwis think immigrants may take their jobs but there is no evidence of this happening because immigrants fill skills gaps.
4. New Zealand has an ageing population and needs younger skilled and educated workers who will contribute to the economy, and immigrants can fill gaps there.
5. Government constantly tweaks policy to make sure it gets migrants with the skills that New Zealand needs.
6. About one percent of the population is made up of immigrants granted permanent residence visas. That is the same as Australia and Canada.



ISBN: 9780170389327

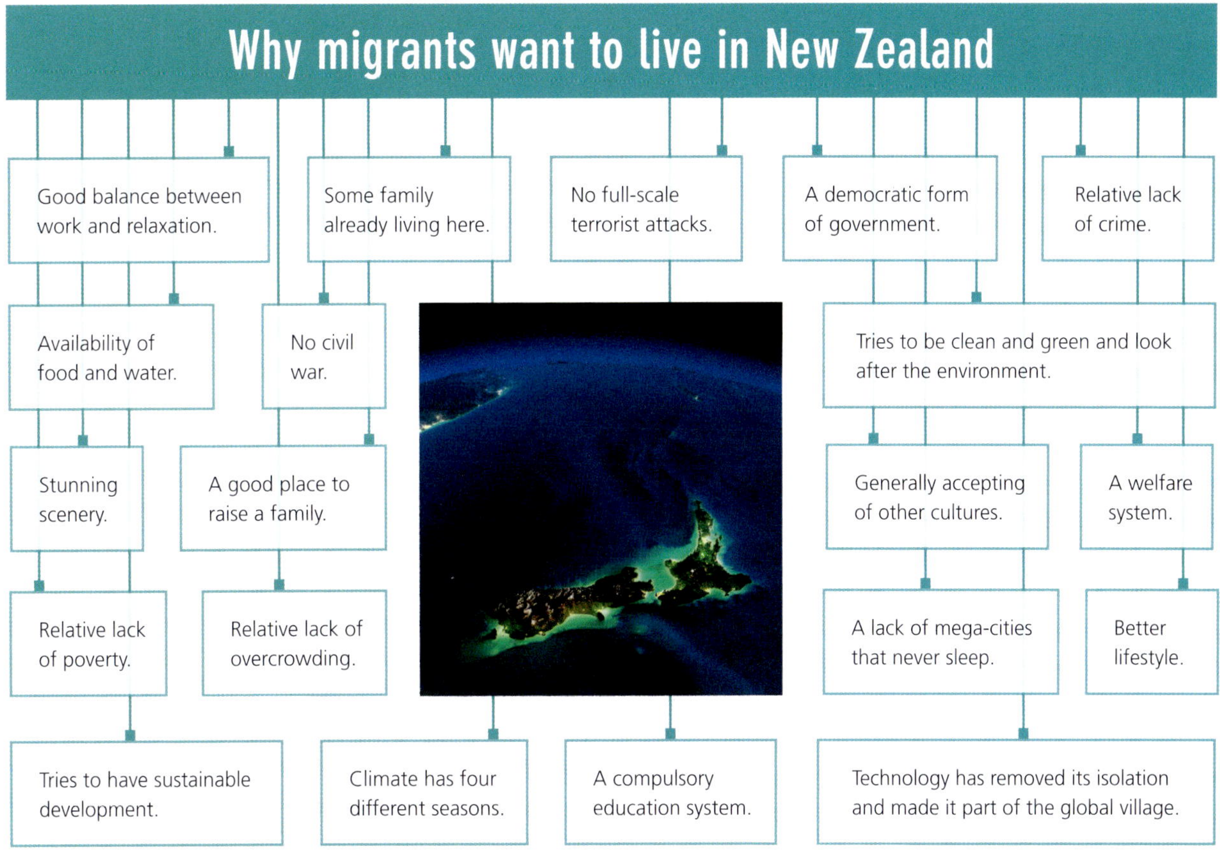


## Views on immigration in one year

### 2016

**NZ First leader** Winston Peters said annual immigration should be capped, migrants should be required to salute the New Zealand flag, people from countries who 'treat their women like cattle' should be interviewed to check their attitude before entry, and because Auckland is facing the same increases as Sydney's house prices, New Zealand should listen to those in Australia calling for Australia to drastically cut immigration.

**Prime Minister** John Key said new migrants bring skills, investment and help for economic growth. The Government was grappling with Auckland's housing market, which had come under pressure partly because of migration and a severe shortage of supply. It recently moved to try to encourage more new migrants to settle outside that region.

The **Finance Minister** said Government might have to bring forward some spending because large migration numbers were driving up demand for public services such as education.

*In 2002, immigration was an important issue in New Zealand's national election. Some people said Prime Minister Helen Clark's Labour Government had allowed immigration to get out of control, that the majority of immigrants approved in recent years had been from Asia and yet Clark had floated the idea of lifting the annual quota of refugees that New Zealand accepted.*

A **Treasury** report suggested immigration was not as good for the country as previously thought and emigration was not as bad as previously thought. Incoming migrants helped the economy by providing skills needed and generally increasing labour market productivity. Although high net migration can contribute to an increase in unemployment and lead to inflation in the housing market, there was no clear evidence yet of skilled migrants contributing to a lack of jobs for local workers.

**Statisticians**, who work out which groups contribute the most to the New Zealand economy after benefits and taxes are taken into account, said in 2016 the group that was contributing most was immigrants from UK and Ireland (nearly $5000). Second was immigrants from Europe and North America ($4500). Third was immigrants from Asia ($2500). Fourth was immigrants from the Pacific Islands ($2000). Last was New Zealand-born citizens ($915).

**Some economists** said that cutting down the number of migrants allowed in could reduce Auckland house prices by a quarter within two years. **The Reserve Bank** told the Government to review immigration policy in a bid to stem house prices. **Government** said there was no need to stem the flow of migrants, that a large proportion of arrivals were returning Kiwis, that high net migration was only one part of a rare trifecta of economic trends.

## SKILLS PRACTICE

1 **Point of View** | What issue is this cartoon addressing and how has the cartoonist expressed his point of view (his attitude) towards this issue?

2 **Demonstrate How to Do Something** | Make some notes on how you would go about demonstrating the following.
   - **a** How to work out what the net migration for a period is.
   - **b** How to show, with the least number of words, the effect of migration on a population over a certain period of time.
   - **c** How to show that people have different opinions on whether or not immigration is good for New Zealand.
   - **d** How to show you understand the *Essential ideas about migration to and from New Zealand*.
   - **e** How to make unbiased comments about why immigrants are attracted to New Zealand.

3 **Background** | Knowing that data has a background story is a useful skill. Study the graph of *Annual permanent and long-term migration* and the background comments, and then do the activities below.
   - **a** Explain what the following mean or represent.
     - **i** The title. **ii** The subtitle. **iii** The source. **iv** (000).
     - **v** Numbers on the *y*-axis. **vi** Numbers on the *x*-axis. **vii** Coloured lines.
   - **b** State things that might be helpful for people to know before they try to analyse data on migration.
   - **c** Explain what would happen if you misread the graph key in a test and thought the orange line was for arrivals.

4 **Appreciation** | Even if you don't like the Bad Driver cartoon, you can still appreciate it. Describe features it has that make it clever and eye-catching.

5 **Selecting** | Select five things, such as a cartoon or an issue, that could serve as a summary of the immigration issue. Name your selections and explain why you selected them.



ISBN: 9780170389327

# 26 Trans-Tasman migration

New Zealand has open migration access with Australia, which means there are few barriers put in front of Kiwis and Aussies who want to migrate across the Tasman.

An Australian nickname for Kiwi migrants is Bondi Bludgers and a comedian said in a Bondi Beach interview, 'To all you New Zealanders, there are only twenty-seven shoplifting days to Christmas.'

A New Zealand Prime Minister said, 'New Zealanders who leave for Australia raise the IQ of both countries.'

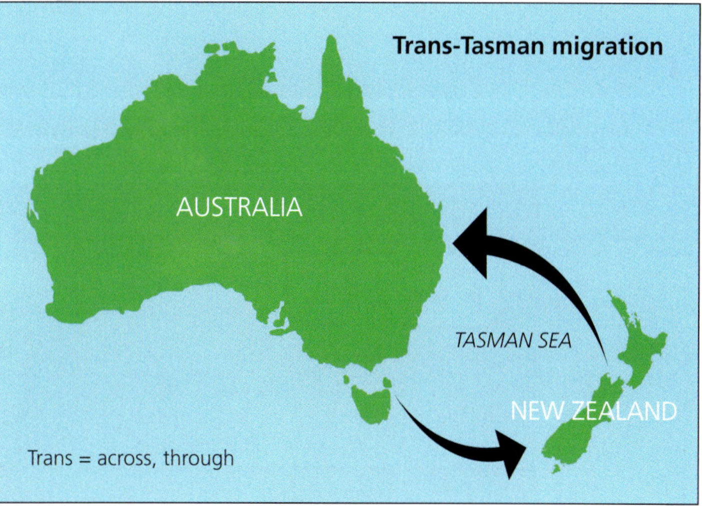


The Australian Government imposed a six-month waiting period before newly-arrived Kiwis could get unemployment benefits and this was later extended to two years. At that time, an estimate said that for every dollar in unemployment benefits paid to New Zealand citizens, the Australian Government got more than $10 in tax from working Kiwis there.

### Push-Pull factors for Kiwi migration to Australia

- Booming mining economy.
- Cheap flights to Australia.
- Higher wages.
- Better working conditions.
- Sunnier climate.
- Other family members already there.
- Similar culture.
- Non-NZ-born people living in NZ could use NZ as 'a back door' into Australia.

### Push-Pull Factors for Kiwi migration back to and Australian migration to New Zealand from Australia

- End of mining boom in Australia.
- Australian high unemployment rate.
- Steady growth of New Zealand's economy.
- New Zealand's falling unemployment rate.
- Wish to help rebuild Christchurch after earthquake damage.
- Building boom in Auckland and other cities such as Tauranga.

### An example of migration data from Statistics New Zealand (June 2015 and June 2016 years)

- A fall in departures to Australia (down 1500) between the two June years, as fewer New Zealand citizens migrated there.
- A net gain of 1900 migrants from Australia in the June 2016 year. June was the ninth consecutive month to show an annual net gain.
- Half of all migrant departures from New Zealand were to Australia during 1979–2016, and seven in eight of these were New Zealand citizens.
- An average of 15,800 New Zealand citizens a year migrated to New Zealand from Australia in June years 2014–16. That compared with an average of 8900 a year in the previous 35 years.
- One in five migrant arrivals to New Zealand in the June 2016 year were from Australia, and two in three of these were New Zealand citizens.
- Australian citizens contributed an average of 3800 a year to trans-Tasman arrivals from 1979 to 2016, although they reached 5000 in the June 2016 year.

ISBN: 9780170389327  

## SKILLS PRACTICE

1 **Practise** | Practise sketching outline maps of New Zealand and Australia and their locations to each other. Then make a good copy. Add names of the Tasman Sea, the Pacific Ocean, Wellington, Canberra, the three islands of New Zealand, and Tasmania. Add some push-pull factors.

2 **Relating Past to Present** | This cartoon is from 2013 when many Kiwis were migrating to Australia. Relate it to the present and say whether or not such a cartoon could be published today.

3 **Speech Bubbles** | Show how the speech bubble in this cartoon presents a reaction to a migration issue.

ISBN: 9780170389327

4 **Opposing Views** | Explain how and why this cartoon presents an opposing view on trans-Tasman migration than the previous cartoon did.

5 **Format** | Comment on what peaks and troughs on a graph mean generally and what the peaks and troughs on this graph mean specifically.

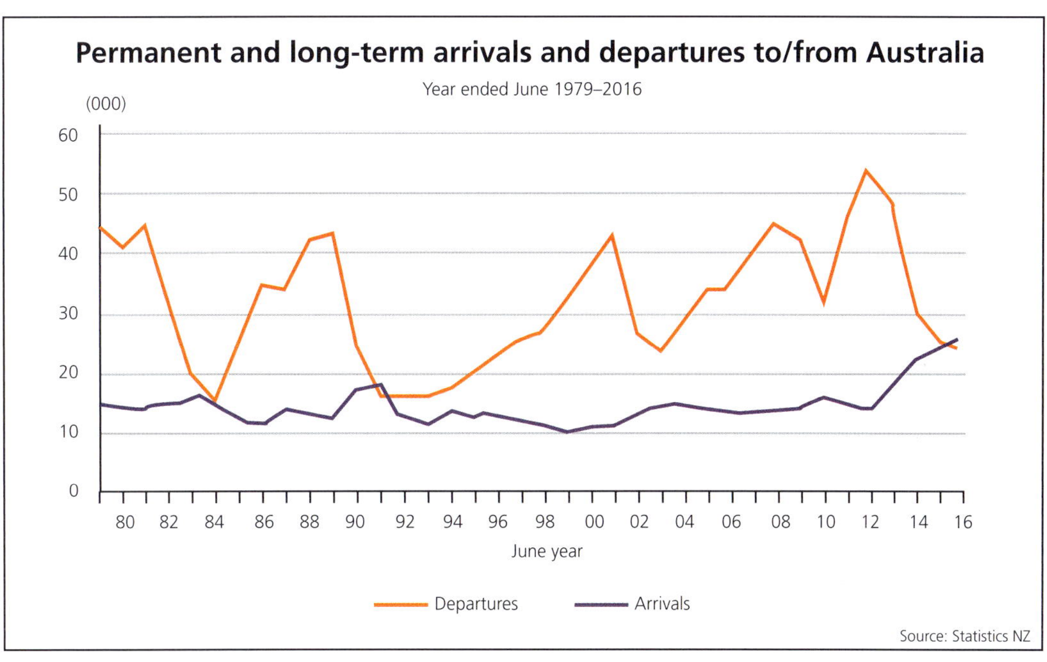

# 27 Transportation was forced migration

Transportation = making people the main cargo in ships that transported them from Britain, where courts had convicted them of crimes such as stealing, to Australia, where Britain had set up penal (punished by law) colonies to house the convicts (convicted people).

*THE LANDING of the CONVICTS at BOTANY BAY*

## The cause

In the 18th and 19th centuries, life in Britain was hard for the poor. Migration from rural areas to the new factories in urban areas had created overcrowded cities and people who had no option but stealing to feed themselves and families.

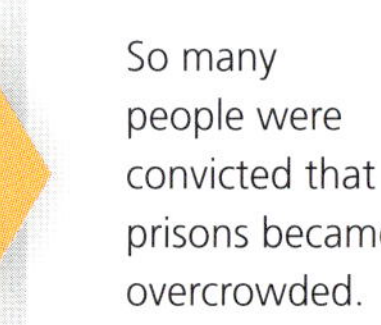

So many people were convicted that prisons became overcrowded.

Prisoners were then kept in old and rotting ships called hulks anchored on the Thames River and in bays.

When the hulks became overcrowded, the British Government decided to set up a penal colony in Australia and transport its convicts there. It thought this would make the punishment for convicts even worse.

## The event

In 1787, the first 700 convicts were transported to Australia and ended up in Port Jackson, now called Sydney. The Governor told convicts that if they wanted to eat they had to work. No relief ships arrived from Britain until over two years later. The British Government kept emptying hulks by transporting convicts to there and to other convict colonies it set up in Australia.

## The results

Transportation had impacts on the sending country (Britain) and the receiving country (Australia).

*Convict in Australia.*

### THE IMPACTS ON BRITAIN

1. It helped to add Australia to the British Empire.
2. It got rid of 162,000 convicts.
3. It broke up families.
4. It did little to stop crime. Transportation did not seem to be such a bad punishment when most convicts chose to stay in Australia rather than come home after they had served their sentences.
5. It became an issue as British society debated whether it was a good thing or a bad thing, and it raised public awareness about systems of punishment.



ISBN: 9780170389327

## THE IMPACTS ON AUSTRALIA

1. When convicts first arrived, Australia had no European infrastructure such as buildings, roads and farms. Most male convicts were young working men with a range of skills in various trades. They were ideal for building European infrastructure and were put to work on public works such as building roads and harbours.
2. Most females were young women who had domestic service skills and were able to have children, thus providing British population to Australia.
3. Australia was a huge country and to keep it the British Government needed colonists to settle the land. Although it encouraged people to emigrate from Britain, few came. So Government offered released convicts free land, tools, seed, livestock and food for one year to settle the land.
4. Most ex-convicts never returned to Britain but stayed in Australia to become landowners or wage workers.
5. This began the creation of a new European society, which eventually led to a nation known for its law-abiding people and low crime rate.
6. The Aborigines had been the only people in Australia for more than 45,000 years. The new land-clearing, building of infrastructure, arrival of diseases, attacks by convicts, and enforced migration to other places impacted on their culture, land and resources.
7. Aboriginal people also impacted on Europeans by sharing knowledge of the land and resources such as finding water, and tracking escaped convicts.

*Billy Blue was convicted for stealing some sugar and sentenced to seven years' transportation. He arrived at Botany Bay in 1801. He married, had six children and became a ferryman in Sydney Harbour and a water bailiff responsible for policing a stretch of water.*

## SKILLS PRACTICE

1 **Empathy** | (Ability to share feelings of another) It is 1787 and you live in England. You have just heard the judge pass this sentence on you: 'The sentence of the court upon you is, that you be transported beyond the seas for the term of fourteen years.'

a Describe how you feel.

b Now study the map of the convict voyage. Describe how you feel at each of the five locations shown by dots.

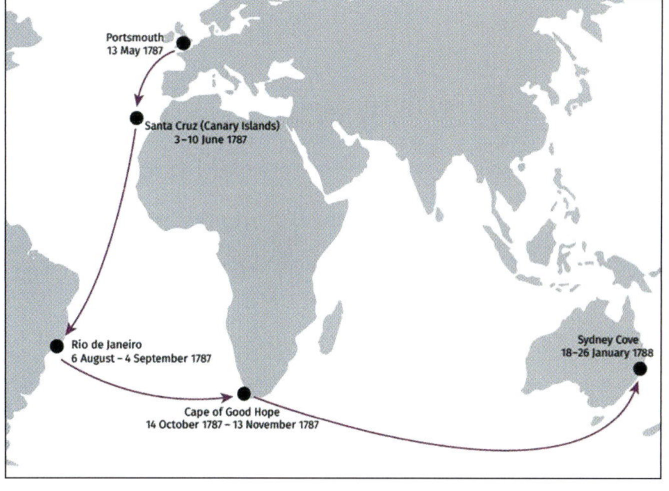


2 **Finding Commonality** | Give the feature that all locations had in common (commonality), the reason for this, and the names of locations not found on the mainland.

**Locations of main Australian penal colonies and settlements**

**Penal colony locations**

1 Sydney Cove 1788
2 Rose Hill 1788
3 Norkfolk Island 1788
4 Coal River, Newcastle 1804
5 Macquarie Harbour, Sarah Island 1822
6 Redcliffe, 1823
7 Moreton Bay, 1824
8 Maria Island, 1825
9 Port Arthur, 1830
10 Cockatoo Island, 1839
11 Swan River Colony, 1850

3 **Diagram** | Create a diagram, such as a fishbone diagram, to summarise the causes and effects of transportation.

4 **Inferring** | Study the graph below and comment on what you can infer from it. Inferring means using your observations to come to a conclusion about something such as when a process may have started or ended.

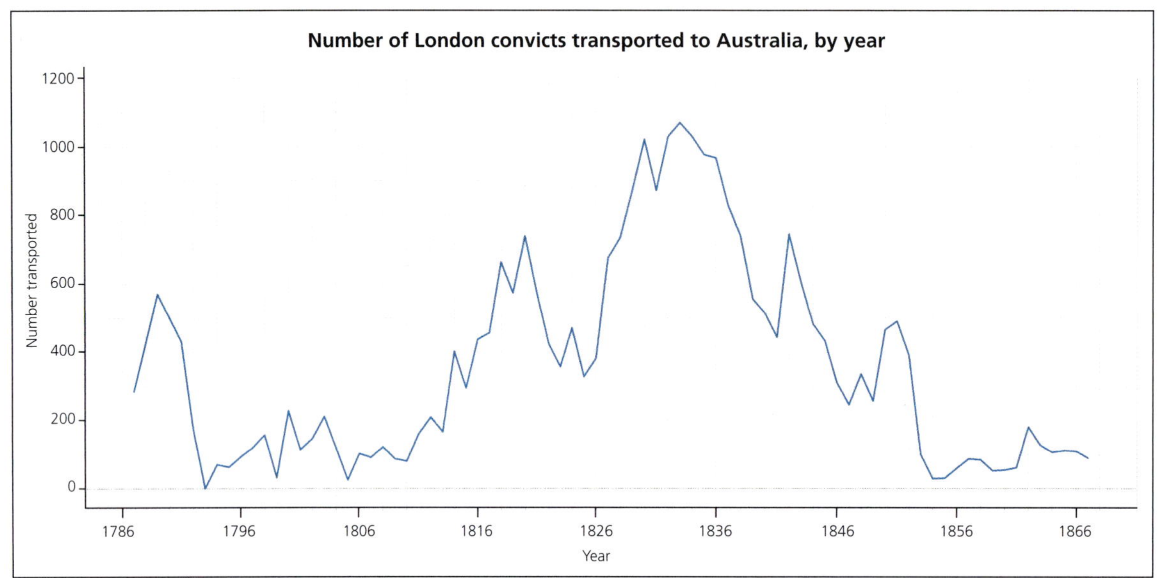


5 **Recalling** | Read the material about Mary Reibey (Haydock) and then close the book. Jot down as many facts as you can about her.

**An example of the progress from convict to valued citizen was Mary Reibey (Haydock) (1777–1855) of England**

She was 13 when she was convicted of horse-stealing and sentenced to seven years transportation. She arrived in Sydney and worked as a nursemaid to serve her sentence. She married Thomas Reibey, a landholder and merchant, and when he died she was left with seven children and many businesses. She became a wealthy and respected businesswoman, with interests in trading vessels and property, and was appointed a governor of the Free Grammar School. Her grandson was Archdeacon of Launceston and Premier of Tasmania. Mary's face is on the Australian $20 note.

ISBN: 9780170389327

# 28 Zero tolerance

Boats bringing human cargoes of asylum seekers trying to get to Australia or New Zealand come mainly from Indonesia. The cargo has often paid a lot of money to people smugglers, and hundreds have died making the dangerous voyage.

Most cargo is people from war-torn countries such as Syria, Iraq and Afghanistan; some is a Muslim minority from Burma.

Australia has welcomed thousands of registered refugees. But it has a controversial policy of zero tolerance towards boats carrying asylum seekers approaching its territory.

In 2015 Australia hit the world news when global human rights organisation Amnesty International said it had evidence showing Australian officials paid people smugglers to turn back a boat to Indonesia with 65 asylum seekers and six crew who claimed to be heading for New Zealand and had GPS that showed they were in international waters when the Australian vessel intercepted them. The crew then transferred the migrants into two smaller flimsy boats, one of which sank near an island in Indonesian waters. The asylum seekers managed to swim to safety. The Australian Government denied the claims. It said, 'It's been a longstanding policy of the government not to comment on on-water matters.' The Prime Minister said his government would do 'whatever we need to do' and was determined to 'stop the boats, by hook or by crook.'

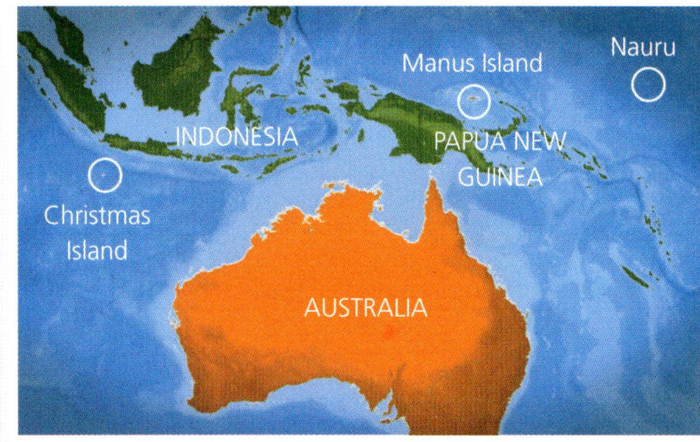


Government has run a campaign to stop asylum seekers. It used coloured advertisements, printed in many different languages. The ads told asylum seekers that: 'If you get on a boat without a visa, you will not end up in Australia. Any vessel seeking to illegally enter Australia will be intercepted and safely removed beyond Australian waters. The rules apply to everyone: families, children, unaccompanied children, educated and skilled. No matter who you are or where you are from, you will not make Australia home. Think again before you waste your money. People smugglers are lying.'

Its military vessels patrol Australian waters and intercept the boats. It has no processing and detention centres for asylum seekers on its mainland but has had such centres on Christmas Island, which belongs to Australia, on Manus Island, which belongs to Papua New Guinea, and on Nauru, which is an independent country. The one on Manus Island got a reputation for violence and in September 2016 PNG and Australia said it was to be closed.

## SKILLS PRACTICE

1 **Cartoon Text** | Study the Hawkey cartoon and answer the questions about it.

- **a** How many text clues are there?
- **b** Which one gives the identity of the cargo?
- **c** Do any suggest from which country the boat most likely left?
- **d** Which ones show the difference between the expected and unexpected destination?
- **e** Which one shows the resolve of the cargo?
- **f** Which one is illustrated by the landscape?
- **g** Which one indicates this cartoon would most likely be from July 2013 rather than October 2016? Give a reason.

ISBN: 9780170389327

2 **Symbols** | Copy the map on page 85 and add symbols representing Australian patrol vessels in the areas you would most likely expect them to be.

3 **Table of Issues** | Study the table and do the following.

a Say what information it gives.

b Say why, if you were doing a piece about the 2015 asylum-seeking controversy, you would need further information than what the table gives.

**Issues concerning Australians 2015**

| Issue | Total press, radio, TV, Net |
|---|---|
| Asylum seeker policy | 41,202 |
| State of origin | 23,244 |
| Pension changes | 8990 |
| Same-sex marriage | 6383 |
| Ron Clarke (Ron Clarke was a famous Australian athlete who had just died.) | 6082 |

4 **Researching a Graphic** | See if you can find one of Australia's NO WAY advertisements and make a comment on how effective you think it is. Note: you are asked to comment on its look, not on whether or not you agree with its intention.

5 **Ranking Evidence** | Study the graph and say how well it explains the following issues. Give it an overall ranking out of 10.

a How Australia's zero policy works.

b Why the policy is considered controversial.

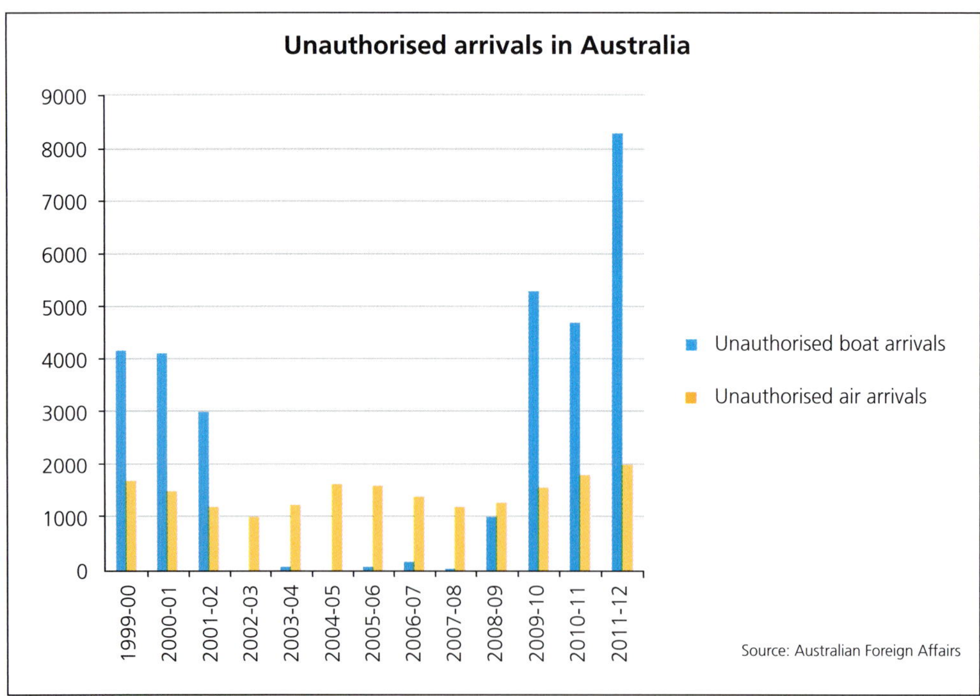


*There is a lack of up-to-date and official information available for migrants arriving in Australia by boat and air.*



ISBN: 9780170389327

# 29 Germans expelled after World War II

*World War II began in 1939 with the Nazis under Hitler, here with his ally Mussolini from Italy, seeking to make his 'German Master Race' rulers of Europe and then the world.*

*World War II ended in 1945 with Germany defeated, Hitler dead by suicide, Mussolini dead by firing squad, and survivors amongst destruction.*

**The Allies, led by the 'Big Three' of Britain's Churchill, USA's Roosevelt and the Soviet Union's Stalin, tried to put Europe together again.**

- Divided Germany into four zones, one each occupied by France, Britain, the USA and the Soviet Union.
- Took away land Germany had captured.
- Redrew boundaries and gave some German land in the east to Poland and the Soviet Union.
- Tried to sort out the problem of 11–20 million displaced people.
- Decided to carry out the largest forced migration in human history by expelling Germans living in eastern Europe and sending them back to Germany. Germans had been living there either because their ancestors had settled a long time ago, or because Nazis had begun to remove groups from those countries and settle Germans in their place.

## Reasons for German forced migrations

1. Wanting to create countries that were not all mixed up with many different groups of people.
2. Thinking expulsion would be the best and most lasting solution.
3. Thinking German minorities in countries may be dangerous in the future.
4. Hoping to get peace in Europe.
5. Punishing Germany whom the Allies said were guilty of war crimes.
6. Avenging the way Nazis had treated people in countries they occupied.

*The Big Three.*

ISBN: 9780170389327  

German and Polish expulsion 1944–48

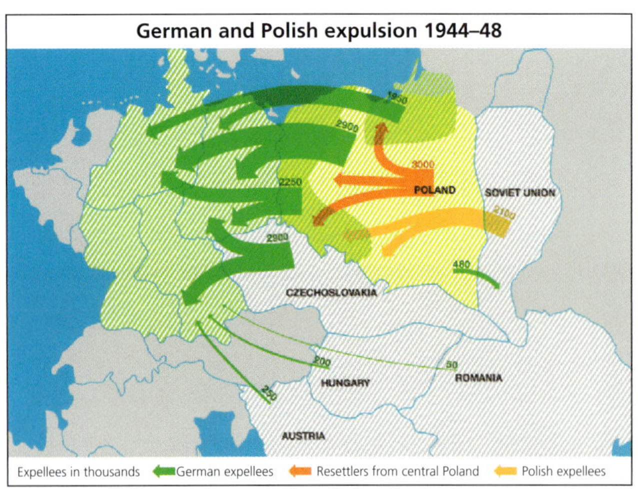


The Allies redrew the map of Poland and shifted borders west. This meant millions had to leave their homes. Poles from the east of Poland, which now belonged to the Soviet Union, were resettled in the west, in old German regions that had now been given to Poland. Germans from there had to move out. Before being removed from the country, they were rounded up by Polish militias and put in camps; many camps were former Nazi concentration camps such as Auschwitz.

**Germany's East Prussia** was divided between Poland and the Soviet Union. Most of its Germans fled west and thousands drowned in overloaded vessels in the Baltic Sea.

**Czechoslovakia** The Allies agreed to the expulsion of the more than 3 million German-speakers.

**Hungary** The Allies agreed to the expulsion of the half-million Germans. They were put on trains and most sent to Germany, but from some villages the adult population was deported to labour camps in the Soviet Union.

**Romania** The Big Three did not give Romania permission to expel its German minorities but Romania did anyway. Tens of thousands of Germans loaded their wagons and hitched their horses to trek to Germany.

**Yugoslavia** The Big Three did not give Yugoslavia permission to expel its German minority but Yugoslavia did anyway. Some were sent to labour camps in the Soviet Union.

## Results

1. Between 1945 and 1950, 12–14 million Germans were forced to migrate.
2. Red Cross officials recorded that life for prisoners inside camps included beatings, rapes, forced labour and starvation diets. Children were also imprisoned, either with parents or in children's camps.
3. Estimates for the number of Germans who died during migrations to Germany range from 500,000 to 2.5 million. Deaths occurred in forced labour camps from doing jobs such as clearing minefields, badly organised evacuations, sinking of refugee ships, long marches in freezing temperatures, attacks by soldiers and civilians, forced marches in which whole villages were cleared at 15 minutes' notice and driven at rifle-point to the nearest border, and in overcrowded and under-provisioned cattle cars of expulsion trains that sometimes took weeks to reach their destination.
4. Declared ineligible by the Allies to receive international relief and lacking accommodation in a Germany wrecked by bombs, many expellees spent time living rough in fields, goods wagons or on railway platforms.



ISBN: 9780170389327

5 Organised massacres of German Jews, called pogroms, broke out in places like Poland and Slovakia. Over 100,000 Jews went to Germany and Austria and most tried to get permission to go to Palestine. The British let in only a few, so Jews stayed in camps. Other surviving Jews from concentration camps who returned to their homes in Germany found they were unwelcome and their homes had new occupants.

6 Many German prisoners of war became forced labourers in other countries to repay destruction that Germany had caused.

## SKILLS PRACTICE

1 **Understanding Europe** | Work out a way you could learn the main countries in Europe and their approximate locations.

2 **Directions** | Explain to what each arrow colour refers on the map at the top of page 88.

3 **Gathering Images** | Find at least five images to do with the expulsion of Germans after World War II and underneath them say what information the image presents.

4 **Placing Images** | Study the three images below and say where you would place them in the text in this unit. Give reasons for your decisions.

*Aachen was the first major German city the Allies occupied.*

*German displaced persons.*

*Allied troops in a German town.*

5 **Context** | The forced migration of Germans is still a disputed issue today as there are no final figures for numbers and some people say it was ethnic cleansing. Make some notes about why other people say it can be important to see events in their context — the setting in which they happened.

ISBN: 9780170389327  

# 30 Aliyah and Nakba

For a while before Israel was created in 1948 the British looked after the area it is in which was known as Palestine. Its 1931 census said the total population was 1,035,154. Of these, 73.4 percent were Muslim, 16.9 were Jewish and 8.6 percent were Christian. The area had places considered holy by all three religions.

For much of their long history, most Jews in the world lived outside Palestine but they often ended religious services with 'Next year in Jerusalem.' The Muslims in Palestine were mostly Palestinian Arabs.

The Jews there wanted their own Jewish state, and the Palestinian Arabs there wanted their own Palestinian Arab state. Both wanted Jerusalem as their capital.

In 1948 Jewish leaders set up a Jewish state there to be called Israel. It said: 'The State of Israel will be open for Jewish immigration and the ingathering of the exiles ...'

The creation of Israel caused two population movements.

1 Jews moved into Israel. This was called Aliyah (ascent).
2 Palestinian Arabs moved out of Israel. This was called Nakba (disaster).

When Israel was created it contained about 1,000,000 Palestinian Arabs. During a 1948 war between Israel and its Arab neighbours that followed the creation of Israel, which Israel won, 700,000–750,000 Arab Palestinians were expelled or fled from Israel to the Gaza Strip, the West Bank, and to the countries of Jordan, Lebanon and Syria.

In 1950 Israel made a law called the Law of Return, which granted every Jew anywhere in the world the right to immigrate to Israel. When Israel declared itself a state, it had about 650,000 Jews in it. During the next three and a half years, 688,000 immigrants came. Aliya continued after that.

## Push and pull factors for Aliyah

- To escape anti-semitism — dislike and discrimination of Jews.
- To practise their religion freely.
- To escape poverty.
- To escape famine.
- To escape political unrest.
- To share their Jewish identity.
- To escape civil war.
- To escape terrorist attacks.
- Israel encouraged Aliyah.
- Israel offered extra help for migrants.

*The city of Jerusalem contains places that are sacred for Jews, Christians and Muslims.*





ISBN: 9780170389327

## Push and pull factors for Nakba

- Jewish military advances.
- Attacks against Arab villages and fears of massacre.
- Expulsion orders by Israeli authorities.
- Voluntary migration.
- Collapse in Palestinian leadership.
- Unwillingness to live under Jewish control.
- In some cases, Arab armies from neighbouring countries, particularly Jordan, encouraged Palestinian towns to evacuate. A possible reason was to stop civilians getting caught in crossfire.
- Israel passed laws after the war to stop Palestinians returning to their homes.

## Palestinian refugees

To house the Palestinians who left, refugee camps were set up in Gaza Strip, West Bank, Syria, Lebanon and Jordan. Camps are plots of land that host governments make available for the United Nations Relief and Works Agency (UNRWA) to house Palestinian refugees. Different sources give different totals for today's Palestinian refugees. UNRWA says there are 5,149,742 registered in total and of these, 1,603,018 are registered in camps; the others live mainly in Jordan and the Palestinian territories.

Efforts by the Palestinian Authority, which governs the Gaza Strip and parts of the West Bank, to create the State of Palestine have been delayed by continuing conflict with Israel and arguments about the Palestinian Arabs who left after the creation of Israel. Some countries recognise the State of Palestine as a state and other countries do not.

## SKILLS PRACTICE

1 **Explaining Clearly** | Explain what the following are, making sure there is no room for misunderstanding of your explanation.

- **a** Palestinian Arab
- **b** Jew
- **c** State of Palestine (Palestine Authority)
- **d** Israel

2 **Special Words** | Give the term for each of the following, and learn the correct spelling of it.

- **a** Hostility towards Jews.
- **b** Migration of Jews to Israel.
- **c** The Arab Palestinians' catastrophe.
- **d** Right of Jews to come and live in Israel.
- **e** City sacred to Jews, Christians and Muslims.
- **f** Governor of the Gaza Strip and in the West Bank.
- **g** United Nations special agency for Palestinian refugees.
- **h** How Jews out of their Holy Land often ended their religious services.

**3 Population Statistics** | Use the table to answer questions about population.

| Population statistics from Israel's Independence Day of 2016 |
| --- |
| Total population = 8,522,000 |
| Jewish population = 6,377,000 = 74.8% |
| Arab population = 1,771,000 = 20.8% |
| First million population = 1949 |
| Second million population = 1958 |
| Projected 10 million population = 2025 or sooner |
| Jewish population growth over past year = 1.7% |
| Arab population growth over past year = 2.2% |
| Number of Jewish people in world = 14.3 million |
| Percentage of world's Jewish people in Israel = 43% |
| Number of illegal migrants in Israel = over 250,000 |
| Migrant arrivals between Independence Day 2015 and 2016 = 36,000 |

- **a** What percentage of Israelis would have been identified as 'Other' in 2016?
- **b** About how many people would that have been?
- **c** What word is used to describe predicted population?
- **d** Which group had the most population growth over the past year?
- **e** Give two statistics that show Israel has legal and illegal immigrants.
- **f** How long did it take Israel's population to go from 1 to 2 million?
- **g** New Zealand's population is expected to reach 5 million in the early 2020s. What might Israel's population be then?
- **h** Out of New Zealand and Israel, which would you expect to have the highest population density, and why?

**4 Comparing Countries** | List similarities and differences between Israel and New Zealand.

**5 Map Creation** | Create a map that shows places where Palestinian refugees live in refugee camps today.

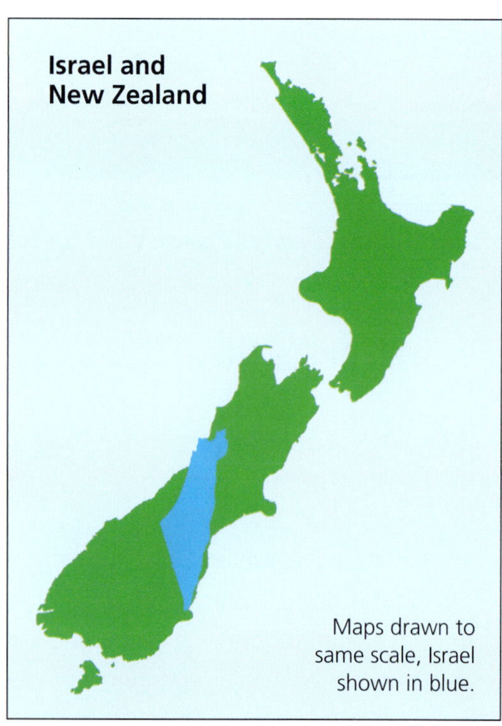




ISBN: 9780170389327

# 31 India becomes two populations

The partition of India caused massive migration.

From 1858 to 1947, the British ruled India. The majority of Indians were Hindu. About 20 percent were Muslim.

In 1947, British rule in India ended and the British divided India into two independent countries. One country was mainly Hindu India, and the other was mainly Muslim Pakistan.

Where the Muslims were living made the partitioning of India complicated. In northern India, Muslims were largely located in two areas on opposite sides of the country to each other. The area between them had mostly Hindus.

This is why the new state of Pakistan had two halves, East Pakistan (today's Bangladesh) in the east and West Pakistan 1700 kilometres away in the west.

Partition was also complicated by the huge numbers of people involved. Before partition, India had about 390 million people living in it. The partition placed about 330 million people in India, 30 million in West Pakistan, and 30 million in East Pakistan.

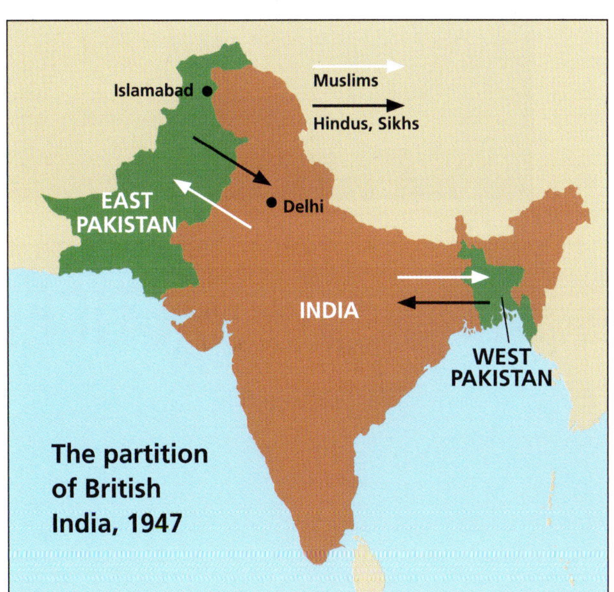


The partition of British India, 1947

Immediately after partition, one of the greatest migrations in human history began. It is estimated that between 12 and 20 million people migrated.

Muslims in the new India went to West and East Pakistan. Hindus, and Sikhs, in the new Pakistan went to India.

Not all Hindus who found themselves now in Pakistan, and Muslims who found themselves in India, migrated; many stayed put.

ISBN: 9780170389327

## Short-term results

- People travelled in buses, in cars, by train, in bullock carts and on foot in great columns.
- Most British troops had been sent home and the Indian and Pakistan troops were disorganised and not prepared for such huge migrations.
- Law and order broke down. Violence erupted between Hindu and Sikh on one side and Muslim on the other.
- Makeshift refugee camps were set up on the new borders.
- Special refugee trains rarely had military escorts so they were easy targets for armed gangs looking to derail trains and stab passengers.
- Poisoned wells meant many migrants had only dirty water such as that from paddy fields. Food was scarce.
- Violence, especially in provinces split between Pakistan and India such a Punjab in the west and Bengal in the east, included crowd attacks on villages and lines of migrants, crowds armed with spears and swords and children armed with sticks, looting, arson, massacres, families split up, abduction of females, mutilation, rape, forced conversion to another religion.
- An official estimate for numbers of abducted women was 50,000 Muslims in India and 33,000 Hindus and Sikhs in Pakistan, but many experts say this estimate is too low.
- Estimates of the death toll during this period range between 200,000 and 2 million.
- There were also stories of friendship between Hindu and Muslims such as a Hindu woman whose Muslim friends were warned by a crowd that if they were still living in the village the next day, the crowd would kill them. The Hindu hid her Muslim friends in a cave outside the village until they could be taken to Pakistan in a protected convoy.

## Long-term results

- Since partition, India and Pakistan have fought three major wars and one minor war over territorial disputes.
- Both countries have tested nuclear weapons.
- Reports of acts of violence on borders continue.
- A special archive has been set up to record oral stories from people who were alive at the time of partition.

## SKILLS PRACTICE

1 **Sketch Mapping** | Draw a sketch map to show the partition of India. Give it a title, colour, key/legend, frame, and arrows to show the directions of migration.

2 **Short-term and Long-term Results** | Explain what the difference is between short-term results and long-term results, using the partition of India as an example.



ISBN: 9780170389327

3 **Numeracy** | Use the data to work out answers to the questions that follow it.

**Example of data used to try to establish migrant numbers**
(Data is deliberately left incomplete here.)

- The 1951 Census of Pakistan identified 7,226,600 displaced people in Pakistan, presumed to be Muslims who had migrated to Pakistan from India.
- The 1951 Census of India identified 7,295,870 displaced persons, presumed to be Hindus and Sikhs who had migrated to India from Pakistan.
- About 11.2 million of the displaced people were in the west.
- 6.5 million Muslims moved from India to West Pakistan, 4.7 million Hindus and Sikhs moved from West Pakistan to India.
- 0.7 million moved from India to East Pakistan, 2.6 million moved from East Pakistan to India.

   **a** How many years after partition were the censuses carried out?
   **b** How many displaced people were identified in censuses of 1951?
   **c** About what percentage of the displaced persons were in the west?
   **d** How many displaced people were in the east?
   **e** About what percentage of displaced people were in the east?
   **f** How many people moved from East Pakistan to India?
   **g** What was the net migration in the east into India?
   **h** How many Hindus and Sikhs moved from West Pakistan to India?
   **i** What was the net migration in the west from India to West Pakistan?

4 **Generalisations** | This primary source gives very detailed and specific data. What generalisations (general ideas) can you make from it?

50,000 Muslims left Amritsar for Wagah. 25,000 Muslims reached Amritsar from Janiala and 20,000 Muslims arrived at Kartarpur from Beas. 40,000 Muslims moved to Kartarpur from Beas … Five abducted Muslim girls were recovered from Anipur in Jullundur area on October 29 in the East Punjab. Troops of the 2nd Asaam Regiment recovered 16 Muslim abducted women and children at Radapur and handed them over to their relatives. Two non-Muslim abducted girls were recovered by Pakistan troops at Ganda Singh Wala, 4 miles west of Kasur, and handed over to Indian troops. At Ravi Bridge, 4 miles south-east of Narowal, 17 non-Muslim women with children were recovered by Pakistan troops and handed over to Indian troops. Families of Royal Indian Navy and Army personnel were moved to India from Sargodha, Multan, Sianvali and Phillawan in Pakistan. (Extract from Press Information Bureau, Government of India. Ministry of Information, New Delhi, 2 November 1947.)

5 **Expressing Opinions** | Give an opinion that each of the following might have expressed on the issue of the partition of India.
   **a** Indian politician who does not want to share power with Muslims.
   **b** British soldier wounded in pre-partition conflict between Hindus and Muslims.
   **c** Muslim male whose sister is abducted as the family moves from India to Pakistan.
   **d** Sikh who lives in Nankana, revered by Sikhs and which becomes Muslim territory at the partition.
   **e** Indian who lives and owns property in Lahore, which becomes part of Pakistan under the partition.
   **f** Member of an armed gang who does not practise any particular religious faith.
   **g** Young Indian who thought before partition that India was headed for civil war because Muslims wanted their own country.
   **h** Hindu couple hidden by Muslim family during massacre of Hindu villagers.

ISBN: 9780170389327

# 32 Vietnamese boat people

Vietnam is a country in what is still sometimes called Indochina, the region of South-East Asia occupied by Myanmar, Cambodia, Laos, Thailand, Malaysia and Vietnam. It is located between India and China — thus Indochina.

Between 1954 and 1975 the Vietnam War was fought between communist North Vietnam and its allies, and non-communist South Korea and its allies. North Vietnam won and Vietnam became one country under a communist government.

The Government then looked to the millions of former South Vietnamese. It carried out executions, put people into re-education camps to turn them into good communists and made them do jobs such as minefield sweeping, and forcibly relocated people to mountain forests to do hard labour. Such actions made many former South Vietnamese determined to get out of the country.

*Some New Zealanders and many Americans fought on the side of South Vietnam in the war.*

Fleeing the country was illegal so migrants could not go by plane. They had to steal away by boat, and so became known as the boat people.

No one is sure how many boat people there were. Estimates say that at least 1.5 million tried to escape, 50,000 to 400,000 died trying to escape, about 800,000 left Vietnam between 1975 and 1995 and arrived safely in another country, and the number of migrants arriving monthly on foreign shores peaked at 56,000 in June 1979.

Even when boats did manage to reach land, some countries in the region, such as Malaysia, turned them away. Some migrants sank their boats offshore so authorities could not tow them back out to sea. Merchant ships, which saw boats in trouble, often refused to pick up the human cargo for fear that no country would let them unload it.

The boats that Vietnamese migrants crowded onto were mostly fishing vessels not designed for open waters and storms. Many people drowned, or died from lack of food and water. Pirates attacked boats, stole possessions, and murdered or sold into slavery their human cargo.



 ISBN: 9780170389327

Western countries agreed to accept 260,000 refugees per year and Vietnam agreed to limit the flow of migrants leaving. Some migrants ended up in refugee camps in Vietnam's neighbours. Most were resettled in developed countries. New Zealand's acceptance of 412 in 1977 was the start of Vietnamese migration to New Zealand.

## SKILLS PRACTICE

1 **Research |** Find at least three pictures of boats that the Vietnamese boat people escaped in and use them as illustrations for a written or oral short presentation about the dangers facing the boat people.

2 **Map Reading |** Study the map and answer the questions about it.

   **a** Describe the shape of Vietnam.

   **b** Explain why Vietnam has been given a different colour to the other countries.

   **c** Why is Vietnam not called a land-locked country like Laos is?

   **d** What is the location of Vietnam in relation to China?

   **e** In which South-East Asian countries did the Vietnamese boat people try to find asylum?

   **f** Why are there no numbers of boat people written on the arrows?

   **g** What group of countries not shown on the map took in boat people?

**Where Vietnamese boat people first tried to find asylum**

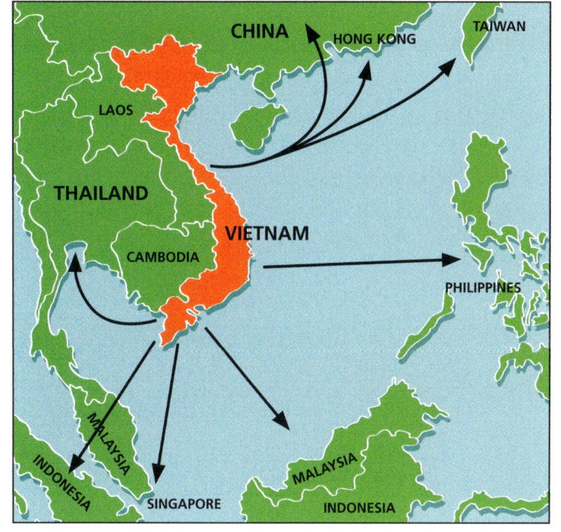


3 **Actions Done and Not Done |** What actions by the Vietnamese Government were push factors for the boat peoples' migration? What actions could the Vietnamese Government have done to persuade the boat people to stay in Vietnam rather than flee?

4 **Links Between Ideas and Groups |** Use the boat people to help you outline possible links among conflict, government and migrants.

5 **Selecting Wisely |** Explain why this photo would or would not be a good one to go with a paragraph you have written about the escaping boat people.

ISBN: 9780170389327  

# 33 Dam causes migration

*China's Yangtze River is the world's third longest river, behind the Nile and the Amazon. Its banks house one-third of China's population and some of the densest population on the planet. Life there had gone on much the same for centuries until the government built a dam, which set off another internal migration in China.*

*The dam is called Three Gorges Dam, after a group of three gorges along the middle reaches of the Yangtze River. The area is about 120 km long and sits in the middle of China. The hydroelectric dam was built in this area near the town of Sandouping, which is in the Yiling District in the city of Yichang in the Hubei province. It took 17 years to build and was finished in 2015. The aim was to produce electricity, increase shipping capacity, and reduce floods downstream. It has also caused massive migration.*

## Migration caused by dam

Officially 1.3 million people were relocated because they had been living in what became the dam's 1045 sq km reservoir.

Experts say the threat of landslides along the dam's banks will force tens of thousands to move again.

Farmers could migrate to newly built cities or stay on farms if they went up to higher ground. But in many villages, too many farmers perched on steep slopes shared too little land.

Farmers who moved upwards cleared land to plant crops or orange trees. This deforestation added to soil erosion, and made hillsides unsafe. In the reservoir region, rising water put more pressure on the shoreline and landslides began on the hillsides. Officials ordered villagers to move.

Thousands of farmers who left were unable to make a living in their new villages and so they returned even though they no longer had residency permits.

People have been relocated all over China — Shanghai, Guangzhou, Tibet, other remote places, and new communities.

Officials said at least four million in one area would have to be moved by 2020 including at least two million living in the reservoir region.

Some communities have not welcomed new migrants.

Government agreed to help displaced people by providing land, jobs and cash compensation. Many people got no compensation or too little. Too poor to buy a city apartment or to build a new home on higher ground, some migrated into tents. Some got moved to small plots of barren land or to urban slums without resources, jobs or housing. There is no official body to hear grievances.



ISBN: 9780170389327

# SKILLS PRACTICE

1 **Location Map** | Study the Three Gorges Dam map and answer these questions.

a What does the darker box on the insert map indicate?

b Which river is most likely to be also called Yellow River and why?

c What word means a lake used as a water supply?

d What word is used for the measurement at the bottom right?

e What is Jialing?

f What does the 'N' at bottom right indicate?

g What symbol is used to show a large urban settlement?

h If Yichang was marked on the map, to which place would it be closest?

i Which city is located on the estuary of the Yangtze?

j Why is migration now linked with the dam site?

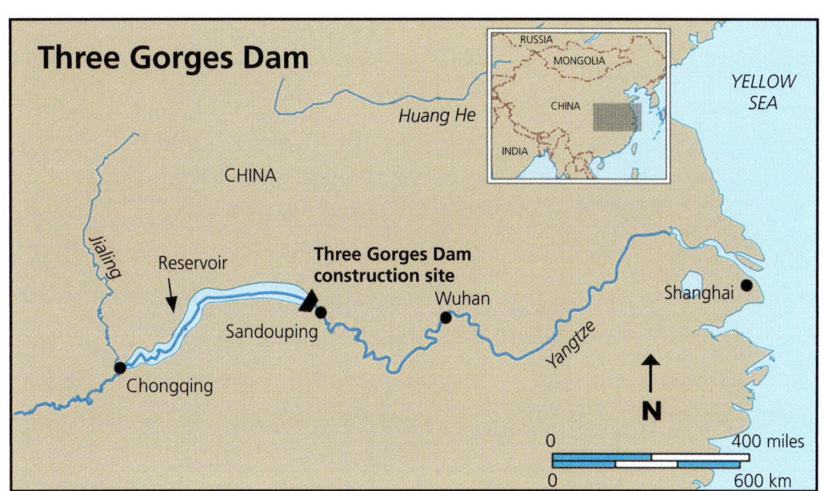


2 **Describing Location** | Describe where the dam is located. A sketch map would be helpful.

3 **Spelling** | Give the correct spelling for the following.

| | | | | | | | | | |
|---|---|---|---|---|---|---|---|---|---|
| a | communnities | b | reservoire | c | officals | d | deforrestation | e | Tibbet |
| f | hiydroelectric | g | Shangai | h | Yungzte | i | compeinsation | j | baren |

4 **Drama** | The Three Gorges Dam drama is still being played out but already there are some obvious actors involved, such as the Chinese Government, and some winners, such as corrupt officials who kept money back from compensation, and losers such as citizens who have to share space with migrants. List all the groups involved.

5 **Perspectives** | Perspectives are particular ways of looking at something and depend on factors such as your age, religion and economic situation. Comment on what perspective on the dam the following are most likely to have.

a The Chinese Government.

b A poor family forced to migrate with no compensation.

c A family who is not forced to migrate and who now gets electricity.

d An honest official who has to get people to move.

e A tourist company manager on the Yangtze River.

# 34 Urbanisation

Urban = to do with cities or towns
Rural = to do with the countryside outside cities or towns
Rural-urban migration = movement of people from the countryside to cities or towns
Urbanisation = an increasing proportion of people living in urban areas
Urban growth = towns and cities cover a greater area of land

Urban processes = inward and outward movements
Inward movement = rural to urban migration
Outward movement = urban to rural migration

- As more and more people migrate from rural villages and farms to towns and cities, urban growth occurs.
- Urban areas have a bigger population density than rural areas do.
- Urban areas include the city or town, whereas rural areas are those that are just near to the city, or surround it.
- Urban areas are more congested in terms of people and buildings than are rural areas.

*Left: Before 1950, rural-urban migration happened mostly in the most economically developed countries (MEDCs) such as England which had set up factories for industries during the Industrial Revolution that took place in Europe and North America in the nineteenth and early twentieth centuries. People from rural areas had migrated to urban areas to work in the new factories. Above: Since 1950, most of the rural-urban migration has happened in LEDCs (Less Economically Developed Countries) in South America, Africa, the Pacific and Asia. It is predicted that 70 percent of the world population will be urban by 2050.*



ISBN: 9780170389327

**Percentage of urbanisation**

| | 1950 | 1990 | 2001 | 2025 |
|---|---|---|---|---|
| **World** | 30 | 45 | 48 | 58 |
| **MEDC** | 53 | 74 | 76 | 83 |
| **LEDC** | 17 | 34 | 41 | 56 |

This has helped cause different levels of urbanisation in countries such as in the table (at right), chosen at random.

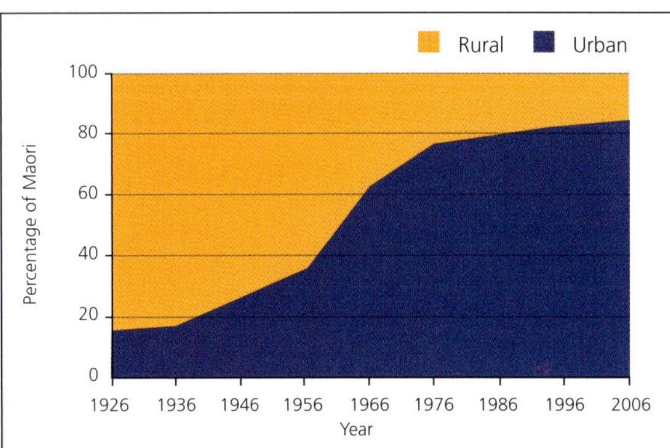


*Movement of Maori to urban areas from rural areas after World War II is sometimes called the Second Maori Migration or the Urban Drift.*

| Country | Urbanisation % of total population |
|---|---|
| Afghanistan | 26.7 |
| Australia | 89.4 |
| Cambodia | 20.7 |
| Egypt | 43.1 |
| India | 32.7 |
| Japan | 93.5 |
| Korea, North | 60.9 |
| Korea, South | 82.5 |
| New Zealand | 86.3 |
| Pakistan | 38.8 |
| PNG | 13.0 |
| Samoa | 19.1 |
| South Africa | 64.8 |
| Uganda | 16.1 |
| United Kingdom | 82.6 |
| USA | 81.6 |

## Cause of rural-urban migration

- Escape from poverty.
- Loss of farmland to land grabbers.
- Pollution or erosion of land.
- Bright lights offer adventure.
- Chance to be anonymous in crowds.
- Better transport.
- Better access to education.
- Better access to health care.
- Escape from tradition (old ways of doing things).
- Escape from family expectations.
- Better marriage prospects.
- Access to better technology.
- Chance to meet a diversity of people.
- More cultural opportunities.
- Better entertainment.
- More opportunities for women.

## Possible results of rural-urban urbanisation

- Fewer rural workers.
- Less food production.
- Less investment in rural areas.
- Shops and services shut in rural areas.
- Growth of mega-cities with over 10 million people.
- Villages lose population and decline.
- Pressure on housing in urban areas.
- Growth of city slums.
- City housing separates into good (often west side) and bad (often east side).
- Pressure on city facilities, e.g. water, sewage.
- Overcrowding in cities.
- Traffic congestion.
- Competition for jobs.
- People cut off from nature.
- City pollution increases.

ISBN: 9780170389327

# SKILLS PRACTICE

1 **Question Creation** | Create 10 questions about this graph that would test a person's understanding of how graphs work.

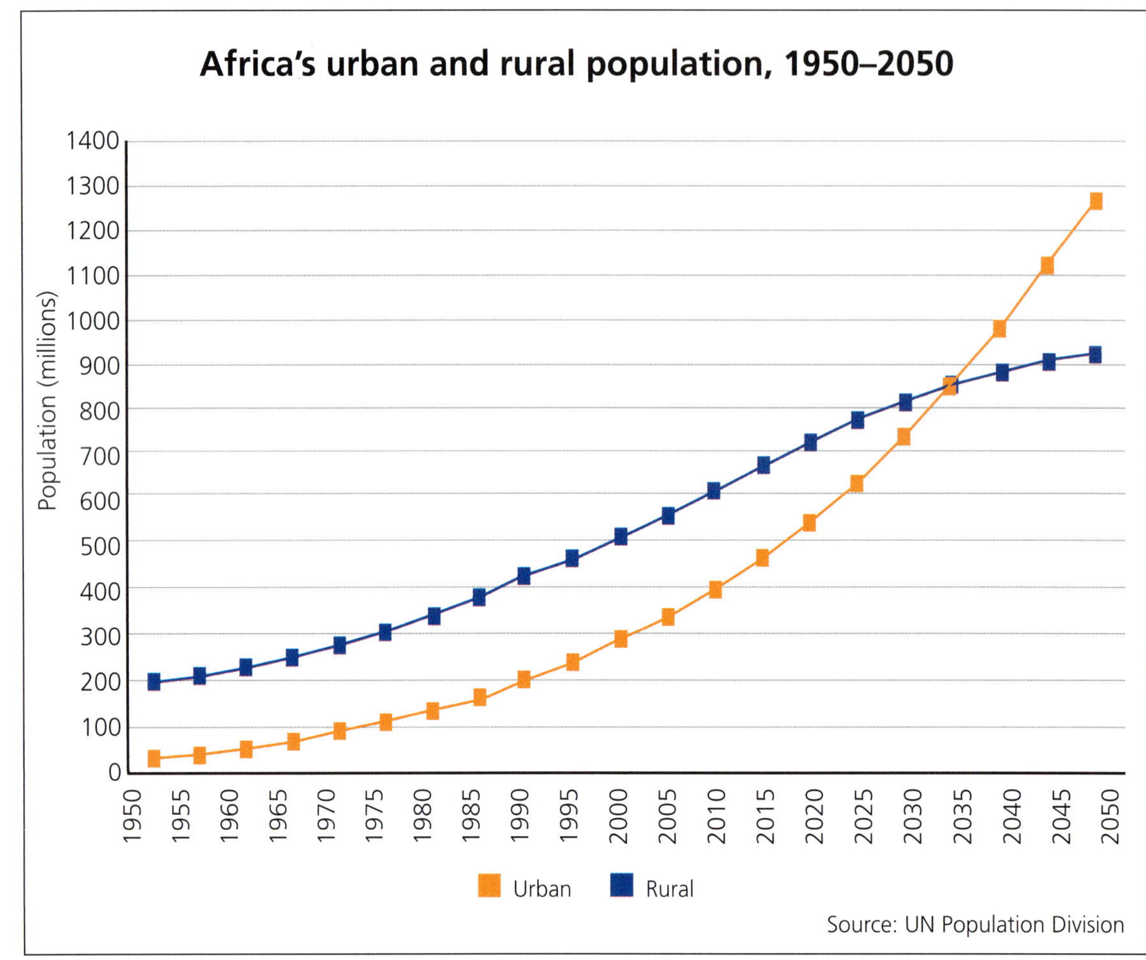


2 **True/False** | Write out the statements below that are true.

- **a** Urbanisation is the increase over time in the population of cities in relation to the region's rural population.
- **b** Industrialisation was a major pull factor in early rural-urban migration.
- **c** Papua New Guinea has a higher urban percentage than does South Africa.
- **d** By 1966, more Maori lived in urban areas than in rural areas.
- **e** Generally, rural areas have a bigger population density than urban areas.
- **f** By 1950, the world's population was evenly split into rural and urban areas.
- **g** Congested means low population.
- **h** The year 1956 was the first time that the Maori urban population equalled the Maori rural population.
- **i** LEDCs stands for Limited Emigration Demographic Countries.
- **j** Urbanisation in the Asia Pacific region is now no longer happening.
- **k** It is predicted that 70 percent of the world population will be urban by 2050.



ISBN: 9780170389327

**3 Visualising** | Visualise (imagine what the finished product would look like) how best to display one of the following statements in the most attention-catching way. Describe your visualisation in words or image.

- In the time taken to read this, the world's urban population has increased by 10 people.
- The 2016 statistics show that at that time the degree of urbanisation in Northern America was 81%, in Latin America and the Caribbean 80%, in Europe 73%, in Oceania 70%, in Asia 47%, in Africa 40%.
- In 1900, 2 out of every 10 people lived in an urban area; in 1990, 4 out of 10 people did; in 2010, 5 out of 10 did; in 2030, 6 out 10 will; in 2050, 7 out of 10 people will.
- In every second, the world's urban population grows by two people.
- In 1800, 3 percent of the world's people lived in urban areas. In 1900, it was 14 percent; in 1950, 30 percent; by 2008, 50 percent.

**4 Multi-tasking** | Study the two graphs and do the activities.

**a** Is 'China's great migration' a suitable title? Give reasons for your answer.

**b** Explain what the Bangladesh graph is showing.

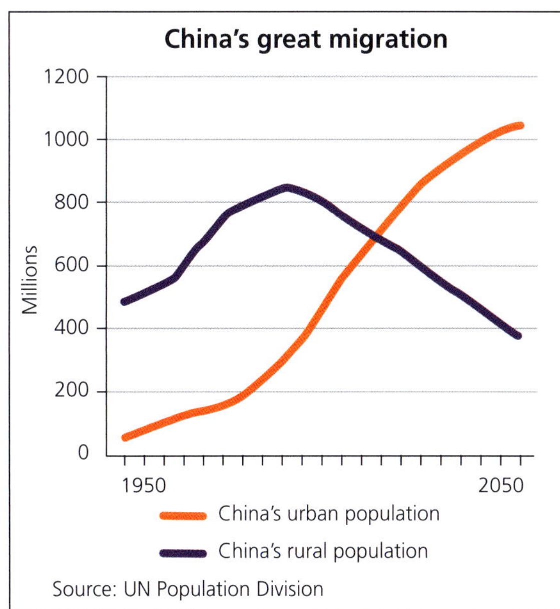


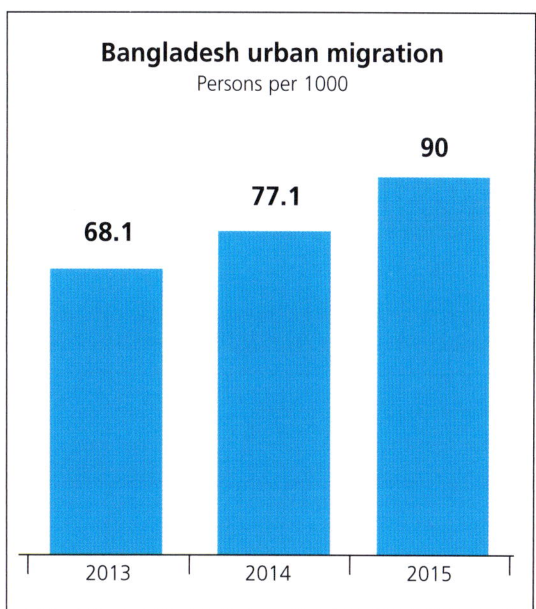


**5 Listing** | List possible results of rural-urban migration for the receiving area and possible results for the sending area.

# 35 Counter-urbanisation

Counter = moving in the opposite direction.
Counter-urbanisation = the process where people migrate from urban areas to rural areas. Since 1950 this process has been happening in MEDCs. Like urbanisation, it is a population movement.

## Reasons for counter-urbanisation

1. Increase in car ownership means more mobility and commuting.
2. Growth in information technology allows working from home.
3. Access to online shopping provides house-deliveries of goods.
4. Problems in urban areas such as crime and traffic congestion.
5. Retired people wanting a quieter lifestyle.
6. New business areas on city edges allows rural living.
7. High urban land values.
8. Lower rural land values and more affordable housing.
9. A more outdoor life and safety for children.
10. Housing developers and estate agents encourage it.
11. Technology such as mobile phones and motorways lessen isolation.
12. Cash-strapped agricultural businesses selling land or buildings.

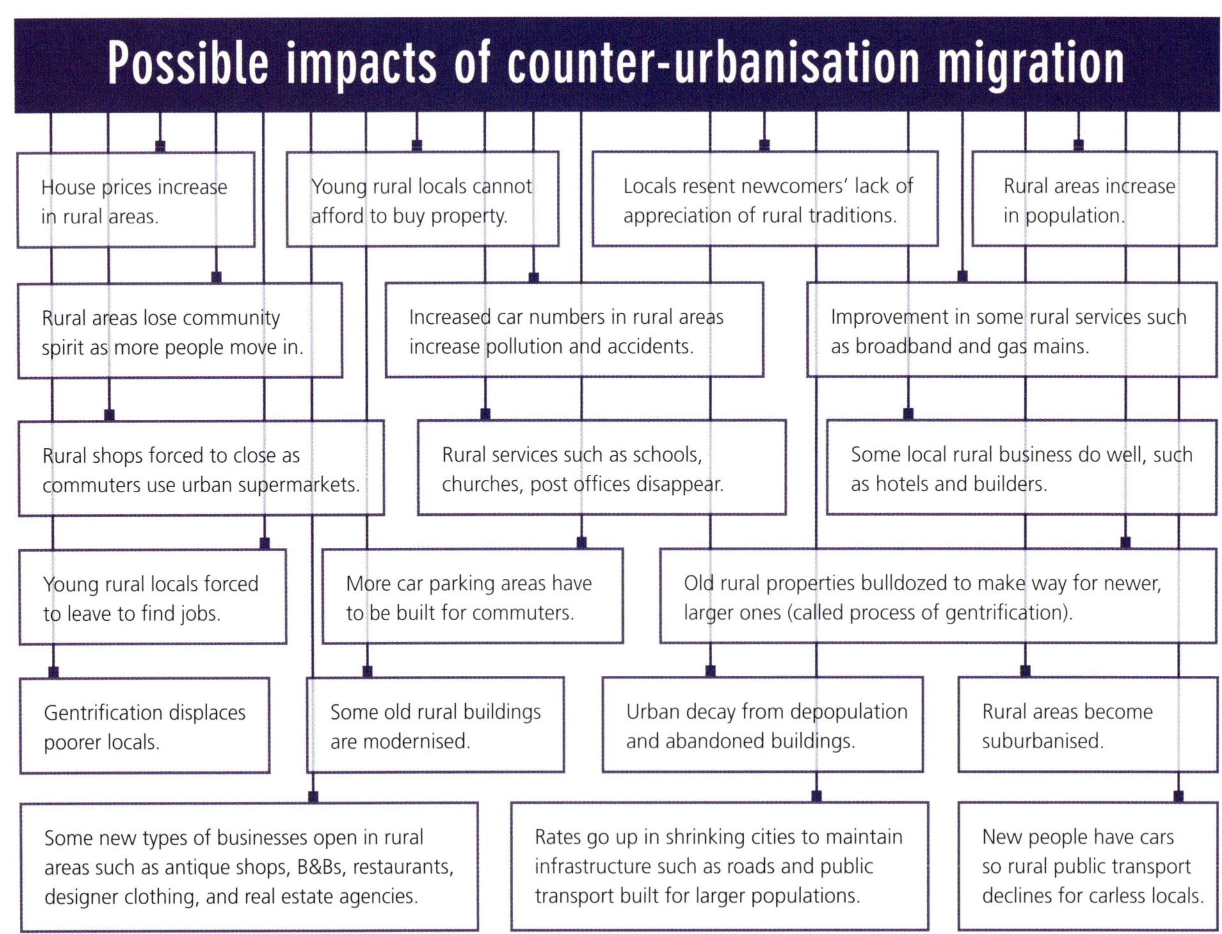




ISBN: 9780170389327

# SKILLS PRACTICE

**1 Describing a Cycle** | Describe how this cycle of rural and urban migration works.

**URBANISATION**
Migration of people from rural to urban areas.

**SUBURBANISATION**
Migration of people into suburbs as urban areas spread out.

**COUNTER-URBANISATION**
Migration of people from urban areas to rural areas.

**RE-URBANISATION**
Migration of people from rural areas to urban areas.

**2 Terms** | Find the meanings of the following terms from the text.

- **a** counter
- **b** MEDCs
- **c** commute
- **d** community spirit
- **e** gentrification
- **f** rural traditions
- **g** infrastructure
- **h** affordable housing
- **i** depopulation
- **j** urban decay
- **k** cash-strapped
- **l** shrinking cities

**3 Weighing Pros and Cons** | You are an 18-year-old about to start a working life and your parents and younger siblings are about to become counter-urbanites. Weigh up the pros (advantages) and cons (disadvantages) of migrating with the family.

**4 Fact Sheet** | Make a single-sheet fact sheet on the results of counter-urbanisation.

**5 Aspects of a Population Movement** | Say to which aspect (part, feature) of counter-urbanisation the following possibly refer.

ISBN: 9780170389327

# 36 Attitudes to immigrants

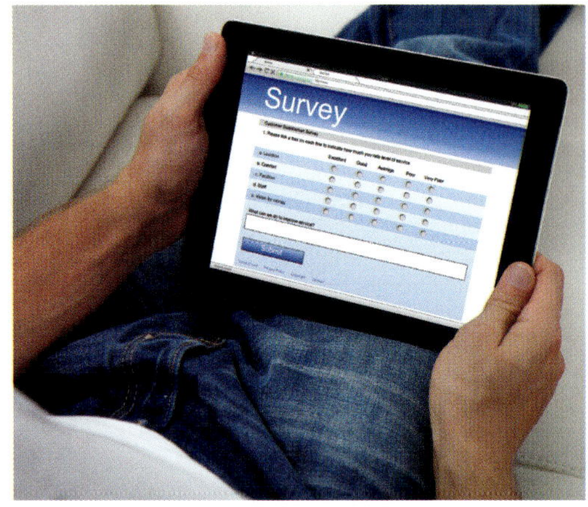


Attitude = a feeling or an opinion about an issue, event, person, thing.

Because migration and migrants are hot issues in countries, many people have definite attitudes about them.

One way to find out people's attitudes is a survey, also called a poll.

It asks people to show attitudes to statements such as 'Migrants make our country stronger because of their work and talents' and 'Migrants are a burden on our country because they take our jobs, housing and health care.'

Colmar Brunton is a market and social research company. A One News Colmar Brunton poll taken in New Zealand in April and in September 2016 asked, 'Do you think the Government should let fewer migrants in, let more in, or is the number about right?'

| The results | April | September |
|---|---|---|
| Should let in fewer migrants | 27% | 38% |
| Current numbers are about right | 51% | 44% |
| More migrants should come | 18% | 13% |
| Don't know | 4% | 5% |
| Among those more likely than average (38%) to say the Government should let fewer migrants in were older people, aged 55 years or more (41%). | | |
| Those more likely than average (13%) to say the Government should let more migrants in were younger people, aged 18–34 years (22%). | | |

## Attitudes affect behaviour

### SOURCE 1

In October 1992 a ship was heading for France with cocoa from Ghana when its Ukrainian crew discovered nine stowaways. They were economic migrants, wanting to get to Europe to have a better life. The crew took all the money the stowaways had and kept them in a compartment for three days. Then they removed them two or three at a time, saying they were shifting them to somewhere more comfortable, but instead throwing them overboard to avoid the fine they would have to pay for bringing illegal migrants into a western port. A 22-year-old stowaway called Kingsley was one of the last two to be removed and he escaped and hid. The crew could not find him. When the ship reached France, Kingsley left his Ghanaian identification papers in a cocoa sack, crept off the ship and went to a police station.



ISBN: 9780170389327

## SOURCE 2

Attitudes make good fodder for political cartoonists. This one from Malcolm Evans appeared in the *New Zealand Herald* in 2002 and features the leader of the New Zealand First Party, Winston Peters, reading stories to children at bedtime.

*Leader of the New Zealand First Party, Winston Peters, reads scary stories to children at bedtime. The scary monster is the Asian taniwha.*

## SOURCE 3

Pegida is a movement founded in Germany in 2014 and has spread to other countries. It wants tighter immigration rules, especially for Muslims.

Supporters of Pegida say: Islam is violent and has increased terrorism in the world. Opponents of Pegida say: That attitude towards Muslims is stereotyping because you can't say all Muslims are the same.

## SOURCE 4

Fortress Europe was a military propaganda term used in World War II for parts of Europe that Nazi Germany occupied. The term reappeared with the European migrant issue when some people said Europe should be a fortress and shut out migrants. The opposing attitude says Europe should not be a fortress against migrants.

## SOURCE 5

In June 2016 people in the UK voted to leave the European Union. A key issue during that time was immigration. Many people said they thought immigration would be better controlled outside the EU than inside it.

A petition that gathered about 217,000 signatures before the vote said: Stop allowing immigrants into the UK. The UK government needs to prevent immigrants from entering the UK immediately! We MUST close all borders, and prevent more immigrants from entering Britain. Foreign citizens are taking all our benefits, costing the government millions! Many of them are trying to change UK into a Muslim country!

## SOURCE 6

Google ran a survey in 2016 over seven days by checking questions users in 21 countries asked. Among the most popular questions were: How to stop migrants? The consequences of letting migrants into Europe? How to volunteer to help migrants? How to adopt a Syrian orphan child?

## SOURCE 7

*The New Colossus* is a poem engraved on a plaque and put inside the New York Statue of Liberty's pedestal. Its most often-quoted lines are, 'Give me your tired, your poor, Your huddled masses yearning to breathe free, The wretched refuse of your teeming shore. Send these, the homeless, tempest-tost to me …'

**Cartoon 1**

*New Zealand Prime Minister in 2005.*

**Cartoon 2**

*New Zealand Prime Minister in 1998.*

## SKILLS PRACTICE

1 **Survey Question |** Create one general question to get an idea of attitudes of people towards immigrants, and survey at least five people. Show the results in a table.

2 **Your Values |** A city you are holidaying in is to be host to a Pegida march and also to an anti-Pegida march. Will you join in and if so, which one? Give reasons for your answer.

3 **Being Logical |** What do each of the following show about attitudes to immigrants?

- **a** The Google questions.
- **b** Kingsley's narrow escape.
- **c** The UK 2016 vote.
- **d** Use of the term Fortress Europe today.
- **e** The UK petition.
- **f** The New Zealand survey.

4 **Compare and Contrast |** Refer to the two cartoons in Source 7 and point out similarities (things they have in common) and differences (things they don't have in common).

5 **Observing and Inferring |** Make a simple line sketch of the cartoon in Source 2 and use boxes and arrows to show some ideas about it. Think of things you can observe, such as actions and use of colour and things you can infer, such as the attitudes.



ISBN: 9780170389327

# 37 Xenophobia

In a week of September 2016, the United Nations held its first-ever summit on refugees and migrants. It was dominated by the war in Syria, which had driven nearly 9 million people from their homes and another 4 million to neighbouring countries or into making the dangerous trip to Europe. The UN Human Rights Chief spoke of 'race-baiting bigots'; the Greek Prime Minister, whose country had had over 12 million migrants cross its borders in the last year, warned that failure to act would unleash xenophobia; and the UN Secretary-General launched a global campaign against xenophobia.

What the people at the United Nations were talking about when they said 'xenophobia' and 'race-baiting bigots' was the dislike, fear, hatred and prejudice of and against migrants who were foreigners to locals.

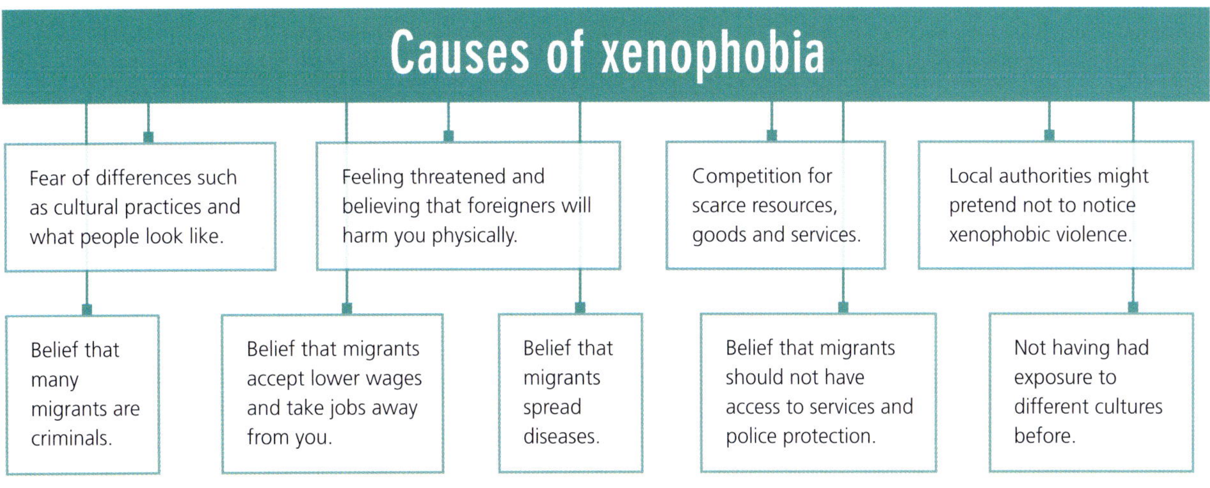


South Africa is often used as an example of xenophobic violence. It is the most industrialised country in Africa and attracts thousands of migrants each year from other African countries and from Asia. Past incidents have involved looting of foreign-owned shops and reports that police helped to raid and loot; Zulu King Goodwill Zwelithini saying foreigners should go back to their home countries after a series of xenophobic attacks such as a Congolese bouncer at a nightclub being doused in flammable substances and then set alight; a Somali shop owner killing a 14-year-old boy during an alleged robbery and triggering waves of attacks against migrant businesses; Ethiopian brothers being critically injured when their shop in a shipping container was set on fire while they were trapped inside; migrants being displaced from torched buildings; cars being set alight; and police firing rubber bullets, stun grenades and teargas canisters in clashes between looters and foreigners.

ISBN: 9780170389327  

In 2016 when Britain voted to leave the EU, anti-migrant feeling was said to be a reason. News headlines at the time included the following:

- Britain must ban migrants
- Migrants handed £1m a week for children back home
- Migrants take all new jobs in Britain
- We must stop the migrant invasion
- There are too many migrants
- 1300 migrants a day pour in
- Send in army to halt migrant invasion
- Migrants send our crime rate soaring.

## Vicious circle

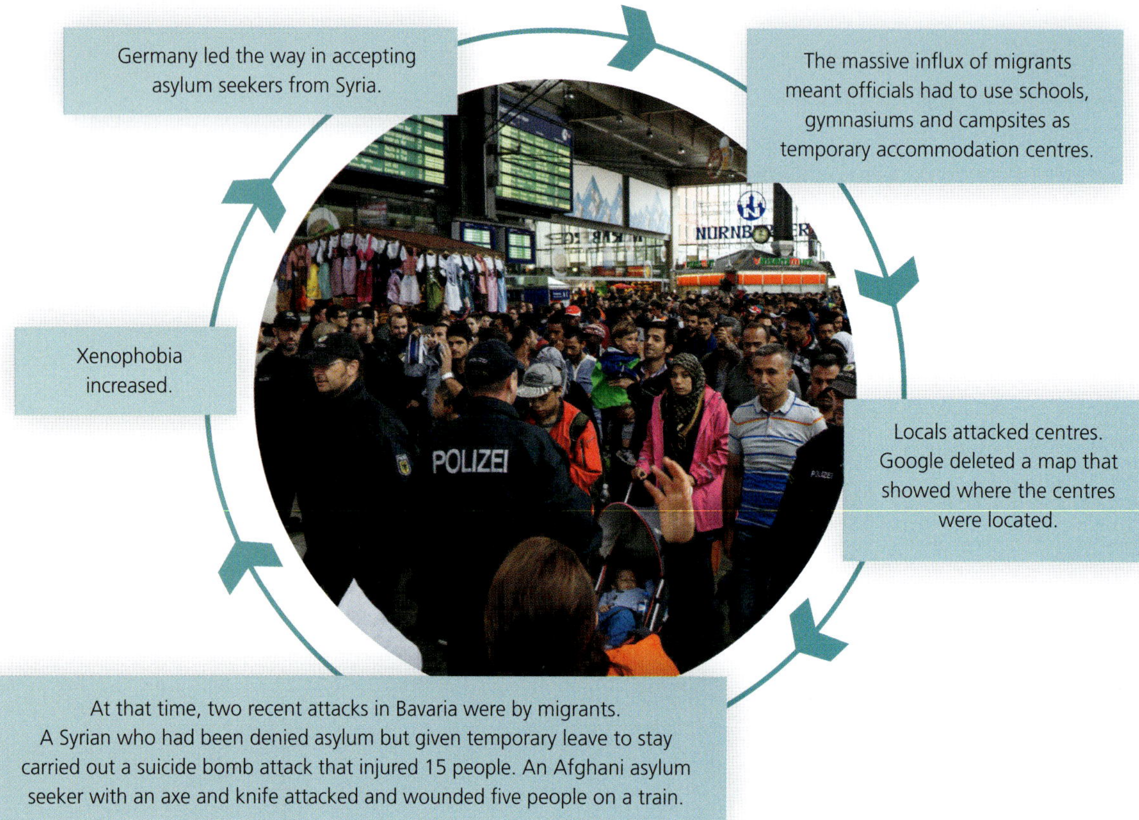

In 2016 Donald Trump campaigned to become president of the US. Critics accused him of xenophobia. He called Mexican immigrants criminals and rapists, and said he would build a border wall between the US and Mexico and make Mexico pay for it. He also called for a 'total and complete shutdown' of the country's borders to Muslims.



ISBN: 9780170389327

# SKILLS PRACTICE

1 **Opposites** | Explain how the sign carries two messages that are opposites.

*Fremdenhass is a German word for xenophobia.*

2 **Understanding Media** | Make some notes you could use in a discussion about why news media report xenophobic violence and don't report a similar number of acts of kindness from locals towards migrants.

3 **Discerning Behaviour** | Say how the following were linked to xenophobia.

- **a** Donald Trump
- **b** The UN Secretary-General
- **c** Google
- **d** British news headlines
- **e** Ethiopian brothers
- **f** Migrant attacks in Bavaria
- **g** The UN Human Rights Chief
- **h** The Zulu King

4 **Preparing Questions** | Prepare at least four questions that will test someone's understanding of this cartoon. It may help to know that some people were saying that comments from New Zealand First Leader Winston Peters about migrants coming to New Zealand were xenophobic.

5 **Applying an Image to Text** | Find words in the image that begin with each of the following letters: b, ste, p, ag, f (five words in all). Supply a clear meaning for each word and then find something in the unit that you could use as an example of the word in action.

# 38 Effects of migration

Migration can bring out the best and the worst in people.

### Example 1

One day in 2016, a young Afghani boy sent a text message from the UK. It said, 'I ned halp darivar no stap car no oksijan in the car no signal iam in the cantenat. iam no jokan valia'. The message went to the cellphone of a woman who was at a New York conference. She and other volunteers at the Calais Jungle had handed out hundreds of cellphones to children, with a number to text in a crisis. She translated the message: 'I need help. The driver won't stop the car. No oxygen in the car. No signal. I'm in the container. I am not joking. I swear to God.' Police in the UK were contacted and they traced the boy's cellphone to a truck in Leicestershire. There they freed 15 migrants. They detained 14 on suspicion of entering the UK illegally and arrested one man on suspicion of human trafficking. They put one child into protective care.

### Example 2

The mass of migrants leaving Syria and trying to get into Europe brought many Europeans with placards out onto streets. Some of the placards had messages such as 'Syrians go home', while some had messages such as 'We welcome refugees'.

## Possible effects of migration on the host country

- Migrants do less desirable manual jobs that locals won't do.
- Migrants fill skills gaps.
- Society gets more cultural diversity, which increases understanding of other cultures.
- New features such as kebab shops.
- Locals get new language skills, which helps for overseas jobs.
- Children in schools don't speak the language of the host country.



ISBN: 9780170389327

- Remittances sent back home means loss of money from host country.
- Increase in population increases pressure on resources and services.
- Segregated ethnic areas created such as Chinatowns.
- Discrimination against migrants can lead to conflict.
- Conflict between those *for* immigration and those *against* it.
- Parents torn between fear of losing children to new culture and their hopes for children to have better lives.
- Young people identify more with peers than with family and this leads to conflict.
- Migrants face culture shock such as learning new language and laws.
- Locals worry about possible terrorism.
- Research shows migrants generally contribute more in taxes and social contributions than they receive in benefits.
- Migrants bring skills and energy.
- Migrants contribute to technological progress and innovation.
- Falling school rolls get boosted.
- Migrants may be exploited.
- Migrants can get a chance of better lives.
- Tourism gets new travel routes.
- Migrants claim police target them unfairly.
- Political correctness such as British councils putting up a festive tree rather than a Christmas tree which might offend Asian and Muslim staff.

## Possible effects of migration on the home country

- Population ageing.
- Economic problems because fewer workers left to support non-workers.
- Lessens the amount of poverty.
- Remittances increase living standards.
- Loss of highly trained people.
- Returned migrants bring new skills such as foreign languages, which helps improve the economy.
- Lessens pressure on resources such as food and social services.
- Reduces population density, which eases overpopulation.
- Returned migrants raise standard of living by expecting better services.
- Marriage rates fall and family structures break down as males migrate.

# SKILLS PRACTICE

1 **Relating** | Relate each image on pages 112 and 113 to a specific effect that migrants can have.

2 **Mind Mapping** | Make a mind map of possible effects of migration generally.

3 **Mihimihi** | Migrants who have escaped from conflict may bring to their new country some personal stresses but also deep gratitude. Use the image on the right to create a mihimihi of yourself as a migrant (basic introduction to tell people where you are from).

4 **Writing a Paragraph** | Choose either the possible effects of migration on the host country or the possible effects of migration on the home country and write a paragraph about it.

5 **Multi-choice** | Migration provides a lot of data for statisticians to translate. Study the graphs and map and create at least two multi-choice questions about each one.

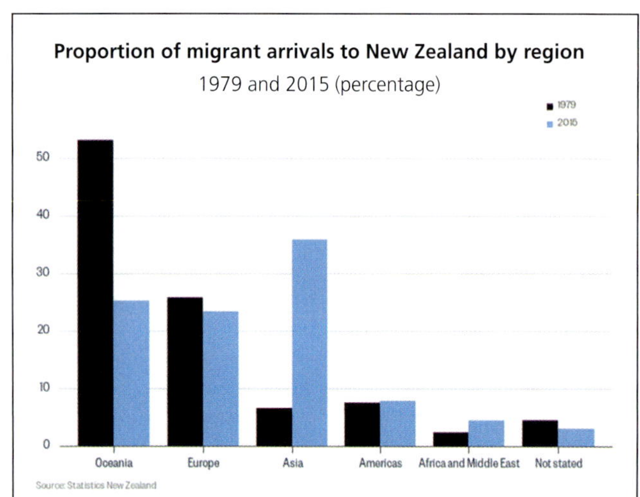


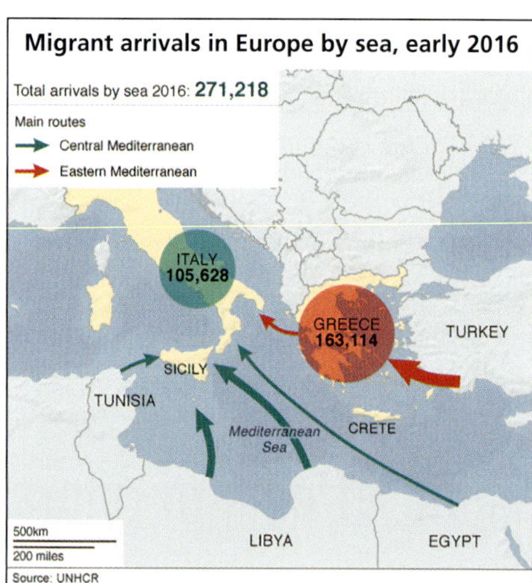


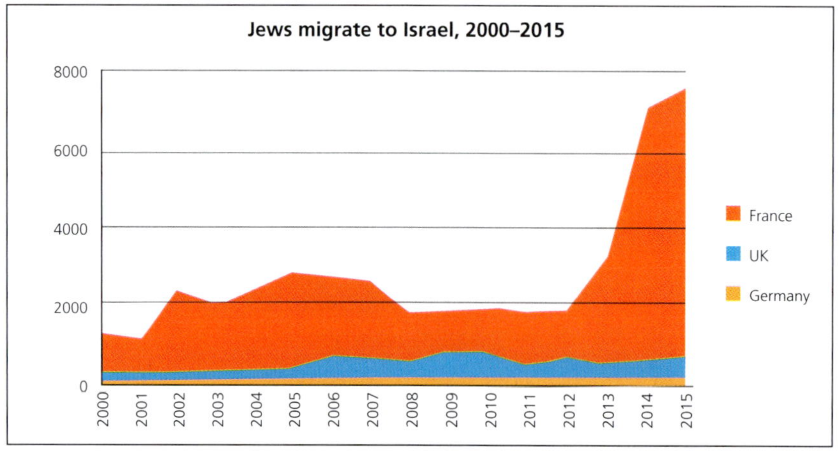




ISBN: 9780170389327

# 39 Future environmental migration

Early people learned to live with their environment. In winter, they wore warmer clothes; in a drought, they cut down water use. Today there are people in the world called environmental migrants or environmental refugees. They are those who can no longer live in their environment because it has changed too much and so they are forced to leave.

## Causes of environmental migration

Droughts that last too long or come too often.

Desertification where land turns to desert and can no longer support people, animals and crops.

Deforestation where developers cut down forests in which people lived.

Sea level rise, which pollutes fresh water and soil, and floods coastal areas.

## The predicted future

The number of environmental migrants will rise as climate change becomes a big push factor.

Migration may affect the environment where environmental migrants go to live, such as straining its resources.

Migration may affect the environment that environmental migrants leave, by allowing it to recover.

### Global warming

- It could create 250 million to a billion climate migrants by 2050.
- UNHCR thinks climate change will be a major challenge.
- The 10 countries with the largest share of populations in low-elevation coastal zones are Bangladesh, China, Egypt, Gambia, India, Indonesia, Japan, the Philippines, Thailand and the United States.
- Millions of people may be forced to leave coastal homes.
- Some island states, such as the Maldives, Tuvalu, Tokelau and Kiribati, will produce many migrants. Governments will have to relocate entire populations.
- Scientists say Bangladesh will lose 17 percent of its land to rising sea levels by 2050, and create 20 million migrants — from just one country.

- Many migrants will come from countries that have contributed almost nothing to climate change affecting them.
- The Maldives is the lowest-lying country in the world. Worst-case current predictions say it will disappear by 2100.

## SKILLS PRACTICE

1 **Photo Evidence** | Study the Maldives photo above and say how it presents evidence that Maldivians might become future environmental migrants.

2 **Projection** | Study the graph of projected (estimated for the future) number of people and give the following information about it.

- **a** The title.
- **b** The source.
- **c** What 'annual' means.
- **d** What is on the *y*-axis.
- **e** Location of the key/legend.
- **f** Reason for two different colours.
- **g** Word used for protection that will be improved.
- **h** Word used for protection that will be unchanged.
- **i** Which type of protection that will cause fewer migrants.
- **j** The names of countries in this unit for which such graphs are important.

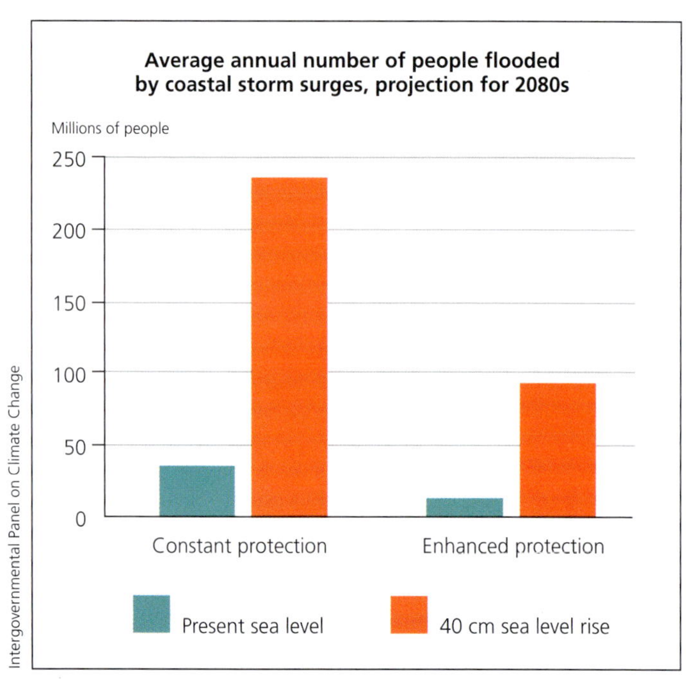




 ISBN: 9780170389327

3 **Language** | Read the following definition of environmental migrants from the International Organization for Migration and rewrite it in more simple language.

'Persons or group of persons who, for compelling reasons of sudden or progressive changes in the environment that adversely affect their lives or living conditions, are obliged to leave their habitual homes, or choose to do so, either temporarily or permanently, and who move either within their country or abroad.'

4 **Selecting** | Select one of the following images to accompany a paragraph you have prepared about future environmental migration. Write a caption to go with your image.

5 **Messages for the Future** | Read the story about Ioane from Kiribati and make some comments about why, although it happened back in 2013, it has some messages for the future.

**Ioane Teitiota from Kiribati**

In 2013, the New Zealand High Court determined the claim of Ioane Teitiota from Kiribati of being a 'climate change refugee'.

*What Ioane said*: He should be allowed to stay in New Zealand even though his visa had expired, because climate change and rising sea levels were destroying his homeland of Kiribati.

*What the judge said*: Ioane should not be allowed to stay, because his case was unconvincing. Kiribati was suffering environmental damage caused by climate change but millions of other people in low-lying countries were in a similar situation. Ioane did not qualify as a refugee under international law because the United Nations definition was that refugees must fear persecution if they returned home and this was not the situation with Ioane who could not argue that the environment was persecuting him. Ioane and his wife moved to New Zealand and chose to stay illegally because it offered a better future than Kiribati. They had three children who were born in New Zealand and they would also be deported because the offspring of illegals born in the country are not recognised as citizens.

# 40 The future

Mass migration from places such as Syria to Europe got people talking about a migrant crisis as if it was something temporary that could be sorted. It will become the new norm because it won't go away or be sorted to please everybody involved.

Mediterranean countries will possibly have to face their own migration in the future. Climate change may force many from Greece, Italy and Spain to move north. One day they could be in refugee camps.

In the 18th and 19th centuries, Europeans such as the British and Dutch set up colonies in regions such as Africa and Asia, and some Europeans migrated there. Today, migration goes from old colony to old mother country, such as Africans to the UK and the Netherlands.

European countries will continue to become more multicultural. This will bring more debate on issues such as wearing burkinis on beaches.

**Projected religious composition of Europe in 2050, with and without migration (%)**

| | With migration | Without migration |
|---|---|---|
| Muslims | 10.2 | 8.4 |
| Hindus | 0.4 | 0.2 |
| Buddhists | 0.4 | 0.2 |
| Other religions | 0.2 | 0.1 |
| Folk religions | 0.2 | 0.1 |
| Jews | 0.2 | 0.2 |
| Unaffiliated | 23.3 | 24.0 |
| Christians | 65.2 | 66.7 |

Rich countries may learn to encourage migration because it is the best way to reduce global poverty. The World Bank says if rich countries let in enough migrants from poor countries to increase their labour forces by three percent, the world would be richer by several billion dollars a year. If rich countries had open borders, it would add trillions of dollars over 25 years to the global economy. It would stop rich countries needing to give money aid to poor countries.

The next big wave of migration will come from Africa. Incomes in some African countries will improve enough to allow people to migrate away from war, natural disasters and bad governments.



ISBN: 9780170389327

Migration will continue because humans still embrace the old saying of the grass is always greener on the other side.

As technologies of communication and travel get better, migration will increase because migrants will have closer contact with families and friends.

Space migration will be essential for human survival in case of an asteroid collision or nuclear war. Space migrants from space settlements will visit Earth for holidays.

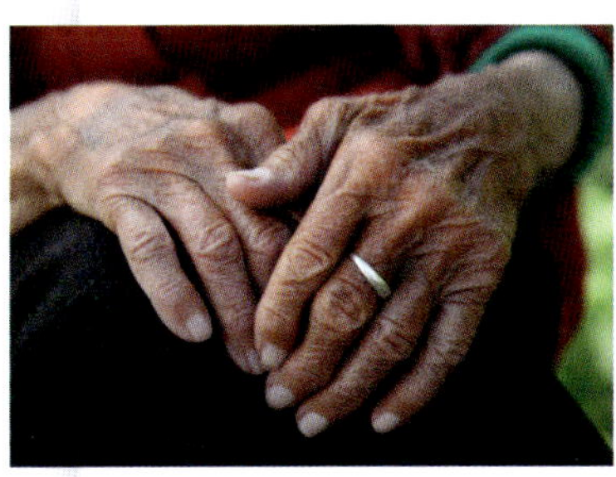

The world's population is getting older. There were 14 million people over the age of 80 in 1950. There will be nearly 400 million by 2050. Fertility is dropping in all regions except Africa. In developed countries, the numbers of people not working will rise and the number of workers needed to support them will drop, while the populations of most developing countries will grow and be young. Only migration will solve the future labour shortage in developed countries, even with robot labour.

Even though the economies of developed countries will move from labour-based manufacturing towards knowledge-based innovation, the demand for highly skilled migrants will rise.

Countries may take notice of things like the 2030 Agenda for Sustainable Development, adopted by world leaders at the United Nations, which asks them to manage migration better and do things such as getting rid of human trafficking.

Globalisation will continue to spread social media, languages and business across borders and will include migrants.

## SKILLS PRACTICE

1 **Word Cloud** | Create a word cloud about migration in the future.

2 **Predicting Population** | Population changes will be important for future global migration. Collect at least six statistics predicting future populations anywhere in the world.

ISBN: 9780170389327

**3 Pairing** | Put two of the following together to create 20 sensible terms to do with future migration.

| | | | |
|---|---|---|---|
| 2030 | aid | Bank | borders |
| closer | contact | countries | countries |
| developed | developing | Development | disasters |
| economy | money | global | highly skilled |
| human | innovation | knowledge-based | labour |
| labour | labour-based | manufacturing | migrants |
| Nations | natural | open | migrants |
| Agenda | population | robot | settlements |
| shortage | space | space | Sustainable |
| trafficking | United | World | world's |

**4 Decision-making** | Think of the good and bad things about being a space migrant and make a decision about whether you would be keen to become one.

**5 Reaction to News Items** | Show how these two news items from the past were related. (Curmudgeon = bad-tempered person) Then comment on whether you would expect similar concerns to be around by the year 2030 and give some reasons for your answer.

**News Item 1**

New Zealand politician Peter Brown, who is himself a migrant from the UK, expressed concern upon learning that New Zealand's Asian population is expected to grow faster than any other, and suggested there are too many Asian migrants in the country. He said, 'The matter is serious. If we continue this open door policy there is real danger we will be inundated with people who have no intention of integrating into our society. The greater the number, the greater the risk. They will form their own mini-societies to the detriment of integration and that will lead to division, friction and resentment.'

**News Item 2**

ISBN: 9780170389327